Grammar and Writing 6

Teacher Guide

Answer Keys and Tests

Second Edition

Christie Curtis

Mary Hake

Houghton Mifflin Harcourt Publishers, Inc.

Grammar and Writing 6

Second Edition

Teacher Guide

Answer Keys and Tests

This edition is based on the work titled *Grammar and Writing 6* © 2006 by Mary E. Hake and Christie Curtis and originally published by Hake Publishing.

Printed in the U.S.A.

ISBN 978-0-544-04428-9

9 10 2266 22 21 20

4500797818 B C D E F G

Contents

To the Teacher

We offer the following suggestions to help you implement the program effectively.

Beginning Class

Notice that each lesson begins with a Dictation or Journal Entry, which students will find in the appendix of their textbooks. To begin their grammar/writing period, students need not wait for teacher instruction, for they will know what to do each day:

Monday: Copy the dictation to prepare for Friday's test.

Tuesday: Write on a journal topic.

Wednesday: Write on a journal topic.

Thursday: Write on a journal topic.

Friday: Look over dictation to prepare for dictation test.

Dictations

On the first school day of each week, students copy a dictation to study throughout the week for a test on Friday. Note the number of words and punctuation marks in the dictation and discuss grammar concepts found in it. To test your students at the end of the week, read the dictation aloud slowly and clearly, allowing time for your students to write the passage with correct spelling and punctuation.

Journal Topics

On Tuesday, Wednesday, and Thursday (non-dictation days), students will spend approximately five minutes writing on a journal topic. We suggest that the student write on these topics in the order they are listed.

Grammar Lessons

Because of the incremental format of this program, Grammar Lessons should be taught in order. Please do not skip any lessons. After reading a lesson, the students will practice the new concept from that lesson. Guide students through the questions in the Practice section and check their answers before they begin the Review Set. Some lessons have "More Practice," which is optional. Some students may need it; others will not.

Grammar Test and Writing Day

We suggest that you give a grammar test after every five lessons. (Notice that the first test follows Lesson 10.) The short, twenty-five question test should allow time for a Writing Lesson to be completed on test day, although you may prefer to teach the Writing Lessons on days other than tests days. Please remember that Writing Lessons are sequenced and should be taught in order. The program is designed so that you do not have a Grammar Lesson to teach on test day. In addition, for the following two or more days you may teach Writing Lessons instead of Grammar Lessons in order to allow students to complete the writing project they began on test day.

On the next page is a suggested schedule for teaching Grammar Lessons and Writing Lessons. Some students might need to spend more than one day on a difficult lesson, so be flexible.

We wish you and your students the best of success. We welcome your feedback at info@studygrammar.com.

Sixth Grade Grammar & Writing Schedule

School Day	Grammar Lesson	Writing Lesson	School Day	Grammar Lesson	Writing Lesson	School Day	Grammar Lesson	Writing Lesson
1	1	1	49	34		96	67	
2	2		50	35		97	68	
3	3		51	test 6	17	98	69	
4	4		52	36		99	70	
5	5		53	37		100	test 13	32
6	6		54	38		101	71	
7	7		55	39		102	72	
8	8		56	40		103	73	
9	9		57	test 7	18	104	74	
10	10		58		19	105	75	
11	test 1	2	59		20	106	test 14	33
12	11		60	41		107	76	
13	12		61	42		108	77	
14	13		62	43		109	78	
15	14		63	44		110	79	
16	15		64	45		111	80	
17	test 2	3	65	test 8	21	112	test 15	34
18		4	66	46		113	81	
19		5	67	47		114	82	
20		6	68	48		115	83	
21	16		69	49		116	84	
22	17		69	50		117	85	
23	18		70	test 9	22	118	test 16	35
24	19		71		23	119	86	
25	20		72		24	120	87	
26	test 3	7	73	51		121	88	
27		8	74	52		122	89	
28		9	75	53		123	90	
29		10	76	54		124	test 17	36
30	21		77	55		125	91	
31	22		78	test 10	25	126	92	
32	23		79		26	127	93	
33	24		80		27	128	94	
34	25		81	56		129	95	
35	test 4	11	82	57		130	test 18	37
36		12	83	58		131	96	
37	26		84	59		132	97	
38	27		85	60		133	98	
39	28		86	test 11	28	134	99	
40	29		87		29	135	100	
41	30		88		30	136	test 19	38
42	test 5	13	89	61		137	101	
43		14	90	62		138	102	
44		15	91	63		139	103	
45		16	92	64		140	104	
46	31		93	65		141	105	
47	32		94	test 12	31	142	test 20	39
48	33		95	66		143	106	

Topical Table of Contents

Sentence Structure

Eight Parts of Speech

Verbs

Spelling Rules

Diagramming

LESSON 1   Four Types of Sentences

Practice 1

  a. imperative

  b. declarative

  c. interrogative

  d. exclamatory

  e. imperative

  f. punctual

  g. considerate

Review Set 1

1. declarative
2. interrogative
3. imperative
4. exclamatory
5. period
6. sentence
7. thought
8. capital
9. question
10. exclamation
11. declarative
12. interrogative
13. imperative
14. exclamatory
15. exclamatory
16. declarative
17. imperative
18. interrogative
19. declarative
20. interrogative
21. imperative
22. exclamatory
23. interrogative
24. declarative
25. punctual
26. considerate
27. The dog likes me.
28. Are you considerate?
29. This is exciting!
30. Try to be punctual.

LESSON 2   Simple Subjects • Simple Predicates

Practice 2

  a. date

  b. character

  c. answer

  d. Dickon

  e. Will succeed

  f. inspire

  g. devised

  h. wrong

  i. moral

More Practice 2   *See answers on page 149.*

Review Set 2

1. subject
2. who, what
3. predicate
4. action
5. sentence
6. leaves
7. squirrels
8. boy
9. Freddy
10. Beth
11. Dr. Monty

12. you
13. She
14. you
15. Were changing
16. sat
17. looked
18. studied
19. speaks
20. can straighten
21. Have traveled
22. is writing
23. Have read
24. Frank has high morals.
25. Is he considerate?
26. I lost my keys!
27. Eat your vegetables.
28. moral
29. punctual
30. considerate

LESSON 3 Identifying Complete Sentences, Fragments, and Run-on Sentences

Practice 3

a. sentence fragment
b. run-on sentence
c. sentence fragment
d. run-on sentence
e. reliable
f. respectful

More Practice 3

1. complete sentence
2. sentence fragment
3. run-on sentence
4. sentence fragment

5. complete sentence
6. run-on sentence

Review Set 3

1. subject, predicate
2. complete
3. fragment
4. subject
5. verb
6. run-on
7. A
8. sentence fragment
9. complete sentence
10. complete sentence
11. run-on sentence
12. complete sentence
13. George Washington
14. Kurt
15. Soltera
16. they
17. reliable
18. respectful
19. moral
20. punctual
21. Do live
22. planted
23. saw
24. gives
25. peacocks
26. Beth
27. Dr. Curtis
28. nurse
29. B
30. B

Practice 4

a. George Orwell . . . book *Animal Farm*. It reveals . . . . [or] George . . . book *Animal Farm*, which reveals . . . .

b. George Orwell was . . . born in 1903. He witnessed the rise of Hitler.

c. One animal character is a boar named Old Major.

d. Bluebell, Jessie, and Pincher are three dog characters.

e. homo-

f. homonyms

g. homophones

h. homonyms

i. homophones

More Practice 4

1. Example: Jayne wrote a poem about promises.

2. Example: Marika loved to read poems by Robert Frost.

3. Example: Emika can write poetry.

4. Example: If you try, you will succeed.

5. Example: An English poet named William Wordsworth captured my interest.

6. *Procrastination* means "putting things off." Don't procrastinate.

7. I procrastinated. I didn't do my work.

8. I'll do it tomorrow. I won't procrastinate.

9. Procrastination steals time. Don't do it.

10. Stop procrastinating. Do your work.

Review Set 4

1. jet

2. weather

3. Turbo

4. landed

5. became

6. caught

7. Sam took his suit to the dry cleaner.

8. The lady wearing a green cape thinks she is a leprechaun.

9. The crew will eat dinner in half an hour.

10. Juan, the ingenious webmaster, created this site.

11. The colonel carried quarters. He had ten.

12. He recognized the dilemma. Then he made a decision.

13. Nancy will fly to Tucson. She has a round-trip ticket.

14. Her ticket is expensive. It costs two hundred dollars.

15. Homophones sound alike.

16. Are you ready?

17. This car has no gas!

18. Don't waste your time.

19. sentence fragment

20. sentence fragment

21. complete sentence

22. run-on sentence

23. homonyms

24. reliable

25. reliable

26. respectful

27. punctual

28. considerate

29. B

30. A

LESSON 5   Action Verbs

Practice 5

a. ruled

b. remember

c. lost

d. declared

e. defeated

f. fought

g. won

h. muttered, whispered, gasped, stuttered, murmured

i. charged, leapt, hustled, skipped, frolicked, dashed, sprinted

j. waist

k. waist

l. waste

m. waste

Review Set 5

1. stung

2. erupted

3. proclaimed

4. stands

5. entered

6. raced, drove, sped

7. trotted, sauntered, clopped, ambled

8. grasps, displays, grips, clutches

9. jogged, ran, drove, flew, stumbled

10. fell, slid, tumbled, ran, biked, stepped

11. homophones

12. homonyms

13. homophones

14. homonyms

15. Grandpa measured the waist of his pants.

16. The waste of natural resources remains a serious problem.

17. Carlos, a respectful student, answered the substitute politely.

18. Izumi is reliable and punctual. [or] Izumi is reliable. She is also punctual.

19. Fernando will travel to Spain. Then he will go to Portugal. [or] Fernando will travel to Spain and then to Portugal.

20. Jakapan enjoys basketball. He also enjoys soccer and . . . .

21. sentence fragment

22. complete sentence

23. run-on sentence

24. sculptor

25. dedicated

26. complete

27. This is boring!

28. Does this story have a moral?

29. Be considerate of others at all times.

30. The Statue of Liberty is wearing a spiked crown.

LESSON 6   Capitalizing Proper Nouns

Practice 6

a. My parents named my sibling Jennifer.

b. Juliet devised a way to be with Romeo.

c. *The Secret Garden* portrays one character as an invalid.

d. The morale of America went down with the depreciation of the U.S. dollar.

e. We attended Arroyo High School in El Monte, California.

f. The Nile River is the longest river in the world.

g. integrity

h. moral

i. honesty

j. dishonor

k. dishonor

More Practice 6 *See answers on page 150.*

Review Set 6

1. Mexico, Florida

2. Henry, Mount Shasta

3. Esther's, Geburah Street

4. Cabrillo Monument, Point Loma

5. December

6. Fridays

7. Laura, Josie's

8. Uncle Jerod

9. *Time Magazine*

10. *A Christmas Carol*, Ebenezer Scrooge

11. integrity

12. dishonest

13. lives

14. assists

15. rushes, walks, runs, hurries

16. bloom

17. interrogative

18. imperative

19. declarative

20. exclamatory

21. Bessie Coleman

22. name

23. served

24. filled

25. sentence fragment

26. run-on sentence

27. complete sentence

28. Bessie learned French and earned money for the trip.

29. On November . . . *Imperator*. It departed . . . .

30. Bessie Coleman received . . . license. She became the . . . black pilot.

LESSON 7   Present and Past Tense of Regular Verbs

Practice 7

a. geology

b. earth

c. geography

d. washes

e. wishes

f. complies

g. tries

h. mopped

i. cried

j. napped

k. raced

l. relied

m. baked

n. sipped

o. dropped

p. pecked

q. talked

Review Set 7

1. reliable

2. punctual

3. integrity

4. waste

5. considerate

6. respectful

7. moral

8. waist

9. homophones

10. homonyms

11. replies

12. buzzes

13. scratches

14. talked

15. rapped

16. tried

17. Niagara Falls

18. *Oliver Twist, David Copperfield,* Charles Dickens

19. Pacific Ocean

20. breach

21. ran, dashed, raced, scampered

22. A person of integrity does not lie.

23. Before painting . . . walls. You should also . . . .

24. complete sentence

25. sentence fragment

26. run-on

27. Barbara

28. requested

29. interrogative

30. exclamatory

LESSON 8   Concrete, Abstract, and Collective Nouns

Practice 8

a. course

b. course

c. coarse

d. concrete

e. abstract

f. concrete

g. abstract

h. audience

i. committee

More Practice 8

1. abstract

2. concrete

3. concrete

4. abstract

5. concrete

6. abstract

7. abstract

8. concrete

9. concrete

10. concrete

11. concrete

12. abstract

13. collection, team

14. flock, bunch

15. family, assortment

Review Set 8

1. leg, truck

2. kindness, liberty

3. club, team, herd, United Kingdom, Central America

4. coarse

5. course

6. course

7. coarse

8. dishonor

9. respectful

10. studies

11. hisses

12. screeches

13. balked

14. trapped

15. fried

16. Barbara McClintock

17. Cornell School of Agriculture, Barbara

18. Barbara, Cold Spring Harbor, New York City

19. Barbara McClintock, Nobel Prize

20. swam

21. glided, raced

22. Dolphins interest me.

23. It takes . . . inhale. They surface . . . .

24. run-on sentence

25. complete sentence

26. sentence fragment

27. surfers

28. measure

29. interrogative

30. declarative

LESSON 9 Helping Verbs

Practice 9

a. is, am, are, was, were, be, being, been, has, have, had, may, might, must, can, could, do, does, did, shall, will, should, would

b. <u>had</u> fought

c. <u>Has</u> helped

d. <u>might have</u> gained

e. <u>must have</u> shared

f. self-discipline

g. willpower

h. self-discipline

More Practice 9 *See answers on page 151.*

Review Set 9

1. is, am, are, was, were, be, being, been, has, have, had, may, might, must, can, could, do, does, did, shall, will, should, would

2. plane <u>should have</u> landed

3. I <u>Shall</u> wait

4. He <u>must have</u> worked

5. Juárez <u>Did</u> help

6. you <u>Do</u> remember

7. you <u>Have</u> memorized

8. James <u>might</u> draw

9. complete sentence

10. sentence fragment

11. run-on sentence

12. Gracie and Lucy are a funny pair.

13. I like to laugh while watching TV.

14. I spoke to each fisherman on the pier at Oceanside.

15. We shall stay. He will arrive.

16. I gathered my books. I left for school.

17. concrete

18. abstract

19. concrete

20. abstract

21. group, committee

22. Do they waste time?

23. Study your geography book.

24. integrity

25. coarse

26. course

27. geology

28. homonyms

29. considerate

30. reliable

Singular, Plural, Compound, and Possessive Nouns • Noun Gender

Practice 10

a. plural

b. singular

c. singular

d. plural

e. father-in-law, chuck wagon, headlight

f. Lucius's

g. Sam's

h. dancers'

i. women's

j. masculine

k. feminine

l. indefinite

m. neuter

n. lay

o. lie

p. lie

q. lay

More Practice 10
See "Silly Story #1" on pages 152–153. Answers will vary.

Review Set 10

1. singular

2. plural

3. plural

4. singular

5. peanut butter, attorney at law

6. Barbara McClintock's

7. sister-in-law's

8. indefinite

9. feminine

10. neuter

11. indefinite

12. is, am, are, was, were, be, being, been, has, have, had, may, might, must, can, could, do, does, did, shall, will, should, would

13. dolphins <u>can</u> communicate

14. you <u>Do</u> know

15. sentence fragment

16. complete sentence

17. run-on sentence

18. Surfers, swimmers, and boaters in the ocean must respect dolphins.

19. Although . . . animals. We should not startle them.

20. concrete

21. abstract

22. abstract

23. concrete

24. South America, school

25. The dolphin is an interesting sea creature.

26. I see it!

27. geography

28. homophones

29. punctual

30. waist

LESSON 11
Future Tense

Practice 11

a. present

b. future

c. future

d. past

e. telephoned

f. will prove

g. talks

h. will

i. shall

j. will

k. shall

l. bio-

m. biosphere

n. Biology

o. biography

Review Set 11

1. past

2. present

3. future

4. will open

5. began

6. pass

7. shall

8. Will

9. plural

10. singular

11. masculine

12. feminine

13. neuter

14. indefinite

15. brother-in-law

16. pharmacist's

17. is, am, are, was, were, be, being, been, has, have, had, may, might, must, can, could, do, does, did, shall, will, should, would

18. quilts

19. <u>would</u> make

20. stitched, sewed, created, designed

21. fragment

22. Annie Dennis . . . mother. She made them . . . .

23. concrete

24. abstract

25. Quilts can preserve family history.

26. Friday, Peter, Paul, Natalee Joe, Phoenix, Arizona

27. lays

28. self-discipline

29. waste

30. geology

LESSON 12   Capitalization: Sentence, Pronoun *I*, Poetry

Practice 12

a. Have . . . "I Have a Dream," . . . Martin Luthor King, Junior?

b. Macavity's a . . . —
For he's the . . . .
He's the bafflement . . . :
For when they . . . !

c. In the year . . . Los Angeles, California.

d. Rules for capitalization are easy!

e. diligent

f. conscientious

Review Set 12

1. Love goes . . .
But love from . . . .

2. *Topiary* is a new . . . .

3. *Topiary,* . . . Latin . . . .

4. In the United States, ...

5. present

6. future

7. past

8. formed

9. will visit

10. shall purchase

11. covers

12. plural

13. singular

14. indefinite

15. neuter

16. boxwood

17. gardener's

18. is, am, are, was, were, be, being, been, has, have, had, may, might, must, can, could, do, does, did, shall, will, should, would

19. gardeners <u>manicure</u> [or <u>shape</u>, <u>trim</u>]

20. Some topiaries are small enough to fit on a table.

21. abstract

22. concrete

23. Do not trample the topiary.

24. conscientious

25. lay

26. Biology

27. Geology

28. biography

29. biosphere

30. willpower

LESSON 13   Irregular Plural Nouns, Part 1

Practice 13

a. bilingual

b. three

c. mosses

d. snakes

e. chimneys

f. bushes

g. Thomases

h. countries

i. bicycles

j. benches

k. days

l. taxes

m. decoys

n. toys

o. cherries

p. babies

q. student's

Review Set 13

1. turkeys

2. pantries

3. perches

4. waxes

5. weasels

6. waxes

7. replies

8. crows

9. ripped

10. brushed

11. dried

12. gentlemen's

13. lawyers'

14. If all the year . . . ,
    To sport would . . . .

15. future

16. present

17. past

18. likes

19. shall taste

20. enjoyed

21. pack

22. (a) feminine
    (b) masculine

23. classroom

24. is, am, are, was, were, be, being, been, has, have, had, may, might, must, can, could, do, does, did, shall, will, should, would

25. mouth <u>does look</u>

26. The squid is . . . fish. It belongs to . . . .

27. democracy

28. geo-

29. uni-

30. moral

LESSON 14   Irregular Plural Nouns, Part 2

Practice 14

a. handfuls

b. mothers-in-law

c. chiefs

d. scarves

e. trout

f. teeth

g. oxen

h. cellos

i. photos

j. cliffs

k. potatoes

l. substitute

m. submarine

n. subsoil

More Practice 14

1. crosses

2. bunches

3. boys

4. lunches

5. bushes

6. losses

7. berries

8. bays

9. sheep

10. men

11. ladies

12. women

13. children

14. mice

15. geese

16. cupfuls

17. wives

18. loaves

19. pianos

20. potatoes

21. fathers-in-law

22. commanders in chief

Review Set 14

1. handfuls

2. brothers-in-law

3. maids of honor

4. cellos

5. solos

6. lives

7. whiffs

8. octopuses or octopi

9. monkeys

10. sentries

11. marches

12. delays

13. faxes

14. buoys

15. ferries

16. lurches

17. tipped

18. players'

19. Friends, Romans, countrymen, . . . ;
    I come . . . Caesar, ...
    The evil that . . . :
    The good is oft . . . .

20. has

21. shall learn

22. touched

23. herd

24. (a) feminine
    (b) masculine
    (c) indefinite
    (d) abstract
    (e) neuter

25. Squids <u>belong</u>

26. feet <u>surround</u>

27. complete sentence

28. unicycle

29. homophones

30. reliable

LESSON 15   Irregular Verbs, Part 1: *To Be, Have, Do*

Practice 15

a. are

b. has

c. does

d. had

e. were

f. did

g. It's

h. its

i. it's

j. its

More Practice 15

1. does

2. has

3. was

4. are

5. were

6. were

7. were

8. are

9. Were

10. Was

11. has

12. Does

13. is

14. is

15. am

16. has

17. has

18. does

19. did

Review Set 15

1. (a) am
   (b) are
   (c) is
   (d) are

2. (a) have
   (b) have
   (c) has
   (d) have

3. (a) do
   (b) do
   (c) does
   (d) do

4. (a) was
   (b) were
   (c) was
   (d) were

5. is

6. had

7. does

8. has

9. passed

10. shall watch

11. blueberries

12. matrons of honor

13. parades

14. altos

15. cupfuls

16. heroes

17. cliffs

18. leaves

19. keys

20. perches

21. clipped

22. ladies'

23. Shakespeare wrote . . . in *Anthony and Cleopatra:*

    I am dying, Egypt . . .
    I here importune . . .
    Of many . . .
    I lay upon thy lips.

24. family

25. squid

26. siphon <u>brings</u>

27. fragment

28. submarine

29. biosphere

30. tri-

LESSON 16   Four Principal Parts of Verbs

Practice

a. (is) listening, listened, (has) listened

b. (is) helping, helped, (has) helped

c. (is) talking, talked, (has) talked

d. (is) proving, proved, (has) proved

e. (is) finishing, finished, (has) finished

f. persevere

g. perseverance

Review Set 16

1. (is) waiting, waited, (has) waited

2. (is) snoring, snored, (has) snored

3. (is) ripping, ripped, (has) ripped

4. (is) drying, dried, (has) dried

5. (is) patting, patted, (has) patted

6. (a) am
   (b) are
   (c) is
   (d) are

7. (a) have
   (b) have
   (c) has
   (d) have

8. (a) do
   (b) do
   (c) does
   (d) do

9. (a) was
   (b) were
   (c) was
   (d) were

10. did

11. had

12. will view

13. shall purchase

14. lived

15. gives

16. torpedoes

17. knives

18. Smiths

19. bogs

20. A brother's murder! Pray can I not.
    Though inclination be . . .

21. salesperson's

22. collection

23. skateboard

24. package

25. I

26. shall appreciate

27. shall

28. declarative

29. It's, its

30. lie

LESSON 17   Simple Prepositions, Part 1

Practice 17

a. aboard
    about
    above
    across
    after
    against
    along
    alongside
    amid
    among
    around
    at
    before
    behind
    below
    beneath

b. beside
    besides
    between
    beyond
    but
    by
    concerning
    considering
    despite

down
during
except
excepting
for
from
in

c. aboard
    about
    above
    across
    after
    against
    along
    alongside
    amid
    among
    around
    at
    before
    behind
    below
    beneath
    beside
    besides
    between
    beyond
    but
    by
    concerning
    considering
    despite
    down
    during
    except
    excepting
    for
    from
    in
    inside
    into
    like
    near
    of
    off
    on
    onto
    opposite

out
outside
over
past
regarding
round
save
since
through
throughout
till
to
toward
under
underneath
until
unto
up
upon
via
with
within
without

d. in, by

e. from, to

f. of, with

g. Throughout

h. out, across, around, past, beyond

i. After, before, along, among, through, during, of

j. among

k. between

l. among

m. between

More Practice 17

1. under, through, to

2. throughout, beneath, among, for

3. Beyond, under, beside, in

4. Inside

5. Without, by

Review Set 17

1. above, after, around, before, below

2. between, but, down, excepting, from

3. of, in

4. At, in, to

5. of, from, by

6. run-on sentence

7. I was climbing high in the tree from branch to branch.

8. (is) wrapping, wrapped, (has) wrapped

9. (a) am
   (b) are
   (c) does
   (d) have

10. (a) was
    (b) had
    (c) did
    (d) were

11. will protect

12. shall share

13. exists

14. examined

15. sopranos

16. halves

17. cuffs

18. sixes

19. Langston Hughes capitalizes . . . poem, "The Negro Speaks of Rivers":

    I bathed . . . Euphrates . . . .
    I built . . . Congo . . . .

20. ran, raced, drove, skipped

21. chair

22. cage

23. mother-in-law

24. tamarins

25. are living

26. (are) living

27. are

28. in, at

29. perseverance

30. coarse

LESSON 18 Simple Prepositions, Part 2

Practice 18

a. inside
   into
   like
   near
   of
   off
   on
   onto
   opposite
   out
   outside
   over
   past
   regarding
   round
   save

b. since
   through
   throughout
   till
   to
   toward
   under
   underneath
   until
   unto
   up
   upon
   via
   with
   within
   without

c. aboard
   about
   above
   across
   after
   against

along
alongside
amid
among
around
at
before
behind
below
beneath
beside
besides
between
beyond
but
by
concerning
considering
despite
down
during
except
excepting
for
from
in
inside
into
like
near
of
off
on
onto
opposite
out
outside
over
past
regarding
round
save
since
through
throughout
till
to
toward
under

underneath
until
unto
up
upon
via
with
within
without

d. With, to, under

e. in

f. to, for, with

g. Until, along

h. From, till, for

i. With, for

j. too

k. two

l. too

m. to

More Practice 18

1. V
2. N
3. P
4. V
5. P
6. N
7. V
8. P
9. N
10. P
11. V
12. N
13. P
14. V
15. P
16. P

17. N
18. P
19. N
20. V
21. V
22. P
23. N
24. N
25. N
26. P
27. P
28. N
29. P
30. V
31. N
32. P

Review Set 18

1. Besides, to

2. by

3. around

4. in

5. After, beneath, with

6. adoration, moral

7. should, have

8. (is) fizzing, fizzed, (has) fizzed

9. may, might, must

10. (a) have
    (b) are
    (c) is
    (d) do

11. (a) did
    (b) was
    (c) were
    (d) did

12. eats

13. will receive

14. sentence fragment

15. Oil spilled . . . ocean. Birds wallowed . . . muck.

16. teeth

17. deer

18. Robert Frost capitalized . . . poem, "Stopping by Woods on a Snowy Evening":

    Whose . . . I think I . . .
    His house . . .
    He will not see . . .
    To watch . . . .

19. somebody's

20. raspberry

21. Meet me at the library.

22. grandparent

23. birds

24. will be examined

25. will, be

26. examined

27. for

28. too

29. among

30. It's

LESSON 19   The Perfect Tenses

Practice 19

a. who's

b. Whose

c. Whose

d. Who's

e. who's

f. whose

g. past perfect

h. present perfect

i. future perfect

j. present perfect

k. completed

l. have

Review Set 19

1. See preposition lists in Lessons 17 and 18.

2. (a) HV
   (b) P
   (c) HV
   (d) P
   (e) HV
   (f) P

3. Since, without

4. future perfect

5. past perfect

6. present perfect

7. will wash

8. does wash

9. will rinse

10. have washed

11. (a) is
    (b) have
    (c) do
    (d) are

12. sentence fragment

13. Jane loved animals. She was a dreamer.

14. (is) persevering, persevered, (has) persevered

15. did

16. works

17. will meet

18. bucketfuls

19. mosquitoes

20. branches

21. keys

22. Langston Hughes wrote this poetry in "Helen Keller":

She,
In the dark,
Found light
Brighter than many ever see.

23. We

24. shall learn; future tense

25. about, of

26. chimpanzees; plural

27. study

28. past

29. too

30. to; to; to

LESSON 20 Capitalization: Titles, Outlines, Quotations

Practice 20

a. I. Grammar lessons
   A. Sentence types
   B. Capitalization

b. *The Call of the Wild*

c. The guide said, "The . . . .

d. The judge stated, "A . . . ."

e. prodigious

f. prodigious

More Practice 20 *See answers on page 154.*

Review Set 20

1. See preposition lists in Lessons 17 and 18.

2. at, on, of, up, for, to, till

3. beneath, of, past, inside

4. (a) *A Wind in the Door*
   (b) *The Adventures of Tom Sawyer*
   (c) *The Lion, the Witch, and the Wardrobe*

5. I. Washing oil-soaked fowl
   A. Use tubs of . . .
   B. Rinse with . . .

6. After Jane Goodall arrived in Kenya, . . . "If . . . Dr. Louis Leakey."

7. present perfect

8. past perfect

9. wastes

10. slipped

11. replied

12. (a) leaves
   (b) wolves
   (c) banjos
   (d) rings

13. plate

14. Please understand me. [or] Understand me, please.

15. (is) wasting, wasted, (has) wasted

16. jet

17. sliced

18. through

19. She flew to Oregon on Monday. She returned on Tuesday.

20. completed

21. Who's

22. among

23. too

24. perseverance

25. its

26. lie

27. course

28. waste

29. bi-

30. homophones

LESSON 21   The Progressive Verb Forms

Practice 21

a. present progressive

b. past progressive

c. future progressive

d. future perfect progressive

e. past perfect progressive

f. present perfect progressive

g. less

h. fewer

i. less

j. fewer

k. less

l. continuing

m. present

Review Set 21

1. In, against, opposite, with

2. punctual

3. considerate

4. Respectful

5. integrity

6. Jane Goodall

7. has been watching

8. has, been

9. (a) fragment
   (b) run-on
   (c) complete

10. In Africa, Jane Goodall . . .

11. She said, "Let us persevere . . ."

12. The book . . . *The Sign of the Beaver.*

13. about

14. hostess

15. bunch

16. (is) talking, talked, (has) talked

17. above, along, at

18. shall

19. will

20. am

21. have

22. boxes

23. sheep

24. future perfect

25. past progressive

26. future progressive

27. present progressive

28. future perfect progressive

29. past perfect progressive

30. (a) progressive
    (b) present

LESSON 22   Linking Verbs

Practice 22

a. is, am, are, was, were, be, being, been
   look, feel, taste, smell, sound
   seem, appear, grow, become
   remain, stay

b. is, am, are, was, were, be, being, been
   look, feel, taste, smell, sound
   seem, appear, grow, become
   remain, stay

c. became

d. was

e. became

f. remains

g. seems

h. appeared

i. no linking verb

j. smelled

k. sympathy

l. compassion

m. sympathy, compassion

More Practice 22

1. seemed

2. remains

3. appears

4. felt

5. remain

6. stayed

7. grew

8. smell

9. become

10. sounded

11. looks

12. is

13. were

14. tasted

15. was

16. action

17. linking

18. action

19. linking

20. action

Review Set 22

1. is, am, are, was, were, be, being, been, look, feel, taste, smell, sound, seem, appear, grow, become, remain, stay

2. is, am, are, was, were, be, being, been, has, have, had, may, might, must, can, could, do, does, did, shall, will, should, would

3. is

4. no linking verb

5. tasted

6. sounds

7. no linking verb

8. appeared

9. (a) during
   (b) except, up

10. William Shakespeare wrote . . . *As You Like It:*
    The fool . . .
    The wise . . .

11. (a) complete
    (b) run-on
    (c) fragment

12. influence

13. has endangered

14. Man's, manatee's

15. has

16. homonyms

17. coarse

18. bilingual

19. between

20. Remember to take out the trash.

21. (a) tablets
    (b) tabbies

22. (is) pitching, pitched, (has) pitched

23. besides, but, down, excepting

24. of, during

25. (a) was
    (b) have
    (c) does

26. past perfect

27. present perfect

28. future perfect

29. had been encouraging

30. are discussing

LESSON 23 — Diagramming Simple Subjects and Simple Predicates

Practice 23

a. siblings | have demonstrated

b. dilemma | caused

c. *Anne Frank: . . .Girl* | portrays

d. Anne | hid

e. attitude

f. morale

Review Set 23

1. waste

2. honor

3. homo-

4. progressive

5. interrogative

6. fragment

7. Christianity

8. branches

9. airplanes

10. turkeys

11. cactuses or cacti

12. Severo Ochoa . . . United States . . . New York University's College of Medicine.

13. I was . . . Dr. Ochoa . . . DNA.

14. Here is an outline:
    I. Severo Ochoa
       A. Physician
       B. Researcher

15. like, of, out, over

16. is, am, are, was, were, be, being, been, has, have, had, may, might, must, can, could, do, does, did, shall, will, should, would.

17. is, am, are, was, were, be, being, been, look, feel, taste, smell, sound, seem, appear, grow, become, remain, stay.

18. belches

19. shall

20. (a) am
    (b) was
    (c) are

21. (is) walking, walked, (has) walked

22. has misbehaved

23. is cooking

24. had been growing

25. action verb

26. linking verb

27. action verb

28. linking verb

29. Gloriana | enjoys

30. Eric | plays

LESSON 24 — Phrases and Clauses

Practice 24

a. clause

b. phrase

c. clause

d. phrase

e. home | is

f. trains | drive

g. James Watt | invented

h. hole

i. whole

Review Set 24

1. lay
2. biography
3. biology
4. uni-
5. declarative
6. complete
7. Mr. Rogers
8. cliffs
9. tomatoes
10. ladies
11. deer
12. There . . . DNA
13. James Watson, an American . . . , and Francis Crick, an English . . .
14. Their . . . , "We wish . . ."
15. since, throughout, to, up, with
16. by
17. hop
18. danced
19. will
20. (a) have
    (b) has
    (c) have
21. (is) finishing, finished, (has) finished
22. had skated
23. was barking
24. will have been practicing
25. action
26. linking
27. clause
28. phrase

29.
scientists	deduced

30.
DNA	has

LESSON 25   Diagramming a Direct Object

Practice 25

a. ideas
b. (none)
c. money
d. capitalism
e.
Industrial Revolution	spread	ideas

f.
United States	practices	capitalism

g. mono-
h. monorail
i. monologue
j. monopoly

Review Set 25

1. submarine
2. subsoil
3. its
4. too
5. imperative
6. exclamatory
7. run-on
8. flock
9. foxes
10. boys
11. lice
12. bluffs
13. Percy Julian . . . Montgomery, Alabama . . . .
14. Soybeans, I . . . .
15. She said, "Percy Julian . . . ."
16. of, of, by, with

17. are, been, have, will, must

18. shipped

19. will

20. (a) does
    (b) do
    (c) do

21. (is) helping, helped, (has) helped

22. will have finished

23. will be going

24. has been planning

25. (a) linking
    (b) action
    (c) linking
    (d) action

26. (a) clause
    (b) phrase

27. cortisone

28.
scientist	synthesized	cortisone

29.
Percy Julian	received	education

30.
Harvard University	awarded	fellowship

LESSON 26   Capitalization: People Titles, Family Words, School Subjects

Practice 26

a. Do, Latin

b. Grandma

c. Have, Dr. Hanfu Lee

d. I

e. conscience

f. conscience

More Practice 26   *See answers on page 155.*

Review Set 26

1. too

2. two

3. to

4. homophones

5. declarative

6. sentence fragment

7. greeting card

8. (a) boats
   (b) banjos
   (c) coaches

9. flower

10. The Flores . . . Paris, France.

11. You . . . Doctor Riggs

12. Kay . . . .

13. I . . . Mother . . . .

14. Is . . . Greek . . . ?

15. above, after, around, before, below

16. what

17. brushes

18. are swimming

19. were nibbling

20. action

21. linking

22. (a) clause
    (b) phrase

23. money

24. no direct object

25. stability

26. shark

27.
Jenny	mailed	letter

28.
Hector	rides	scooter

29.
Fins	help	shark

30. | fin | provides | movement |

LESSON 27 Descriptive Adjectives

Practice 27

a. positive, positive

b. thankful, pleasant

c. abstract

d. black-and-white

Answers e–g will vary; see examples below.

e. lovable, shaggy

f. sudden, loud

g. patient, weary

h. affect

i. effect

More Practice 27
See "Silly Story #2" on pages 156–157. Answers will vary.

Review Set 27

1. perseverance

2. prodigious

3. Whose

4. who's

5. interrogative

6. run-on

7. religion

8. (a) crunches
   (b) Sundays
   (c) commanders in chief

9. Mr. Van Genderen . . . House of Representatives.

10. Here is an outline:
    I. Friends
        A. Holly
        B. Laura

11. beside, beyond, by, down, excepting

12. should, would

13. is, am, are, was, were, be, being, been, look, feel, taste, smell, sound, seem, appear, grow, become, remain, stay

14. mopped

15. has demonstrated

16. will be leaving

17. action

18. linking

19. phrase

20. clause

21. progressive

22. perfect

23. | Wright Brothers | opened | shop |

24. | brothers | built | glider |

25. inexperienced, dangerous

26. cheerful

27. lovable

28. salty

29. filthy

30. fearless, new

LESSON 28 The Limiting Adjective • Diagramming Adjectives

Practice 28

a. feint

b. feign

c. faint

d. faint

e. Kristen's, several

f. Some, people's

g. This, two, that, three

h. Jeremy's

i.

```
Jeremy | enjoys | class
                    \his  \music
```

More Practice 28   *See answers on page 158.*

Review Set 28

1. monologue
2. whole
3. less
4. fewer
5. imperative
6. complete sentence
7. congregation
8. (a) cuffs
   (b) candies
   (c) pailfuls
9. The . . . I . . . .
10. Grandma Hoppy . . . .
11. into, of, on, out, round
12. of, off, on, onto, opposite, out, outside, over
13. are, being, may, could, have
14. what
15. continuing
16. (a) have
    (b) have
    (c) has
17. have demonstrated
18. have been studying
19. linking
20. action
21. clause
22. phrase
23. no direct object

24. attention
25.

```
Cleo | read | newspaper
```

26.

```
Chico | swam | mile
```

27. (is) feigning, feigned, (has) feigned
28. an, a, the
29. Some
30.

```
strawberry | stained | hand
 \This \sweet \red        \her
```

LESSON 29   **Capitalization: Areas, Religions, Greetings**

Practice 29

a. In . . . *The Lion, the Witch, and the Wardrobe,* C. S. Lewis . . . Aslan . . . Jesus Christ.
b. When I . . . South, I . . . .
c. Please . . . .
d. Dear Mom,
      I miss you so much.
                  Your daughter,
                  Maria
e. incredible
f. believe
g. incapacitate
h. incapacitate

Review Set 29

1. faint
2. conscience
3. mono-
4. monorail
5. continuing
6. interrogative
7. complete sentence
8. Pacific Ocean

9. (a) hoboes or hobos
    (b) syllabuses or syllabi

10. My . . . Becky . . . .

11. Irene's . . . English, French . . . .

12. The son . . . Little League . . . .

13. Hey, Dad, may I . . . ?

14. Was the Union Army . . . North . . . South?

15. Go . . . Methodist church

16. The . . . "Dear Ms. Johnson," . . . "Gratefully, Mrs. Strobel."

17. through, till, toward, until, upon

18. work

19. are, be, taste, appear, become

20. (a) am
    (b) are
    (c) were

21. had worked

22. had been experimenting

23. (a) action
    (b) linking

24. (a) phrase
    (b) clause

25. (is) affecting, affected, (has) affected

26. No, the, the, two

27. This, my, Felix's

28.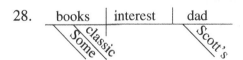

29.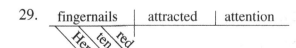

30.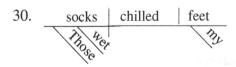

Practice 30

a. Swiss (cheese), American cheese

b. Victorian era

c. Boston (cream) pie

d. New York drivers

e.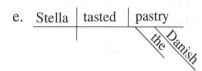

f. capital

g. capital

h. Capitol

i. capital

j. capital

Review Set 30

1. incredible

2. incapacitate

3. effect

4. affect

5. completed

6. exclamatory

7. run-on sentence

8. truth

9. chalkboard

10. (a) salmon
    (b) ditches
    (c) messes

11. Tigger, Winnie the Pooh . . . Eeyore . . . A. A. Milne's *Winnie the Pooh*.

12. like, with, on

13. do, does, did

14. slide

15. (a) do
    (b) does
    (c) did

16. shall have discussed

17. will have been playing

18. action

19. linking

20. clause

21. phrase

22. (is) incapacitating, incapacitated, (has) incapacitated

23. The, flamboyant, red, curly

24. No

25. that

26. Easter basket

27. American flag

28. British people

29.

30.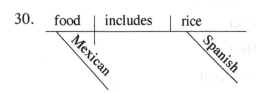

LESSON No Capital Letter
31

Practice 31

a. depend

b. Independence

c. injustice

d. no additional capital letter

e. no additional capital letter

f. English

g. Wise . . . .

h. Thirty-four . . . .

More Practice 31 *See answers on page 159.*

Review Set 31

1. hole

2. monopoly

3. feign

4. morale

5. exclamatory

6. run-on

7. wallpaper

8. plate

9. gulfs

10. loaves

11. Is . . . ?

12. Surfing . . . Pacific Ocean . . . Atlantic Ocean.

13. phrase

14. through, throughout, till, to, toward

15. am, were, being, must, will

16. seem

17. were, look, appear

18. buzzes

19. (a) have
    (b) had
    (c) have

20. talk, (is) talking, talked, (has) talked

21. continuing

22. present

23. present

24. linking

25. action

26. red-colored

27. an, a

28. Danish scientist

29.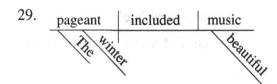

The winter pageant | included | music
                                      beautiful

30.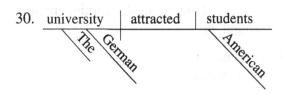

The German university | attracted | students
                                        American

LESSON 32 — Transitive and Intransitive Verbs

Practice 32

a. transitive, <u>grated</u>, *cheese

b. intransitive, <u>flew</u>, no direct object

c. transitive, <u>Did answer</u>, *phone

d. intransitive, <u>was named</u>, no direct object

e. after

f. postscript

g. postgraduate

h. postwar

i. postmortem

Review Set 32

1. conscientious

2. It's

3. under

4. compassion

5. declarative

6. complete

7. completed

8. have

9. intransitive

10. transitive

11. pity

12. cookies

13. sheep

14. altos

15. The

16. *Charlotte's Web,* Charlotte, Wilbur

17. clause

18. before, behind, below, beneath, beside, besides, between, beyond, but, by

19. may, might, must

20. look, feel, taste, sound, smell

21. pried

22. polish, (is) polishing, polished, (has) polished

23. action

24. linking

25. no direct object; intransitive

26. sites, transitive

27. Horseback, sandy, dry

28. This

29. Tataviam people

30.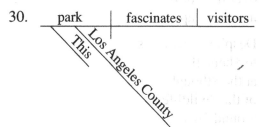

This Los Angeles County park | fascinates | visitors

LESSON 33 — Object of the Preposition • The Prepositional Phrase

Practice 33

a. about noncommunicable *diseases

b. by human *contact or airborne *microbes

c. from *parent
   to *child
   through their *genes

d. to the next *generation

e. oar

f. or

g. ore

More Practice 33

1. for *miles
along the *levee
through historic *battlefields
beyond the *suburbs
of *Princeton

2. past some *golfers
at a country *club
by a ferocious *dog
without a *leash

3. After an *hour
with a *sigh
of *relief
toward *home

4. At the *end
of her *run
in the *woods
at the *edge
of the *water

5. With inquisitive *eyes
over the *bridge
near her *apartment

6. Despite *weariness
to *herself
at the *thought
of the *wildlife
around *her

Review Set 33

1. capital

2. capital

3. Capitol

4. capital

5. exclamatory

6. fragment

7. congregation

8. tree's

9. gentlemen

10. heroes

11. Twenty-one, Geraldine's

12. Tourists, Gulf of Mexico, Pacific Ocean

13. phrase

14. aboard, about, above, across, after,
against, along, alongside, amid, among,
around, at

15. in a big *box
with *string

16. Until *sundown
around the *lake
over the beaver *dam
with the *current
against the *current
through enemy *territory

17. of *bones
with *holes
in *them

18. write

19. looked

20. shall

21. have discovered

22. was playing

23. action

24. linking

25. no direct object, intransitive

26. holes, transitive

27. popular, single-reed

28. two

29. New York City orchestra

30.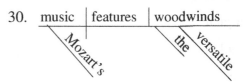

LESSON 34 — The Prepositional Phrase as an Adjective • Diagramming

Practice 34

a. picture *of a young skeleton*
bones *of cartilage*

b. <u>ends</u> *of bones*

c. <u>material</u> *inside our ears and noses*

d. of all your bones, names

e. in the upper leg, bone

f. Without ligaments, skeleton

g.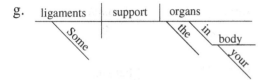

h.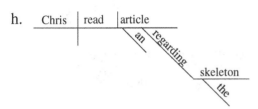

i. poor

j. pore

k. pour

l. pore

Review Set 34

1. postgraduate

2. postwar

3. postscript

4. injustice

5. interrogative

6. complete

7. United Nations

8. volleyball

9. arches

10. maids of honor

11. In

12. Do I

13. clause

14. of, off, on, onto, opposite, out, outside, over

15. Amid the *confusion
    in the *key

of *C
with *no one
besides *Caleb
until *midnight

16. in modern science, formula

17. has, have, had

18. appeared

19. (a) are
    (b) are
    (c) were

20. will have been teaching

21. will have guided

22. linking

23. action

24. no direct object, intransitive

25. truths, transitive

26. great, unelected

27. His

28. American scientists

29.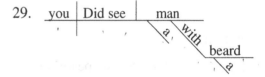

30.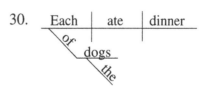

LESSON 35   Indirect Objects

Practice 35

a. dialogue

b. dia-

c. diameter

d. diagonal

e. driver

f. owner

g. guests

h. no indirect object

i.
```
policeman | issued | ticket
                \(x)
                  \driver
```

j.
```
dog | brought | newspaper
            \(x)
              \owner
```

Review Set 35

1. poor
2. pore
3. oar
4. ore
5. declarative
6. run-on
7. indirect
8. President's Day
9. stallion
10. handfuls
11. toys
12. The, Bengal
13. King Lear, William Shakespeare's *King Lear*
    I
    More
14. phrase
15. under, underneath, until, unto, up, upon
16. for *cooking
17. from Ecuador, bananas
18. can, could
19. tastes
20. (a) do
    (b) does
    (c) do
21. had been growing
22. (a) linking
    (b) action

23. no direct object, intransitive
24. bananas, transitive
25. zookeeper
26. elephant
27. Some
28.
```
monkey | threw | banana
   \The            \the
```
29.
```
you | Have seen | banana
                 \a  \on tree
                      \a
```
30.
```
gorilla | picked | orange
 \The \frisky  \(x)me  \an
```

LESSON 36   The Period, Part 1

Practice 36

a. I. Children's literature
   A. Picture books
   B. Modern fantasy and humor

b. She read *The Swiss Family Robinson* by J. D. Wyss.

c. Don't be insensitive.

d. Reading different types of books is fun.

e. prudence

f. discretion

g. discretion

Review Set 36

1. dia-
2. diameter
3. or
4. post-
5. preposition
6. adjective

7. indirect

8. direct

9. complete sentence

10. elephant's

11. mice

12. vetoes

13. monkeys

14. Lake Erie . . . Great Lakes.

15. The . . .
    I. Book report
       A. Plot
       B. Characters

16. Some . . . South . . . .

17. clause

18. of *them

19. is, am, are, was, were, be, being, been, has, have, had, may, might, must, can, could, do, does, did, shall, will, should, would

20. love, (is) loving, loved, (has) loved

21. had loved

22. have been making

23. That

24. period

25. period

26. exclamation

27. period

28. period

29. present

30.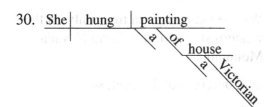

LESSON 37   Coordinating Conjunctions

Practice 37

a. and, or, for, so

b. but, nor, yet

c. and, but, or, nor, for, yet, so

d. yet

e. or

f. but

g. for, and

h. sow

i. sew

j. so

Review Set 37

1. discretion

2. independence

3. postmortem

4. persevere

5. transitive

6. object

7. continuing

8. fragment

9. chorus

10. professor

11. deer

12. fathers-in-law

13. The House of Commons, Great Britain

14. Huck Finn, Miss Watson

15. First, Ms. Smith's Daniel, David, Derrick, Doug

16. concerning, considering

17. in *length

18. of the national tree contest; winner

19. <u>Do</u> know

20. <u>shall have</u> washed

21. <u>had been</u> growing

22. shall go

23. Some, a, giant

24. Redwoods date back 100 million years.

25. Let us protect the redwoods.

26. I. California's state trees
    A. Coast redwood
    B. Giant sequoia

27. coordinating, conjunction

28. and, but, or, not, for, yet, so

29. or

30.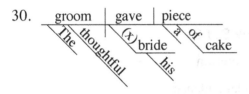

LESSON 38 Diagramming Compound Subjects and Predicates

Practice 38

a. their

b. They're

c. there

d. they're

e.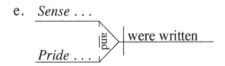

f.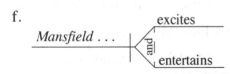

g.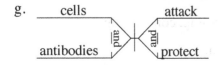

More Practice 38 *See answers on pages 160–162.*

1. so

2. Homonyms

3. aren't

4. integrity

5. present

6. imperative

7. Labor Day

8. pigs

9. foxes

10. tankfuls

11. Snakes

12. Aunt Nova

13. The, Dear, Dr. Camiling, Gratefully, Mrs. Hernández

14. aboard, about, above, across, after, against, along, alongside, amid, among, around, at

15. of *bones
    for one *snake

16. are

17. were

18. is, am, are, was, were, be, being, been, look, feel, taste, smell, sound, seem, appear, grow, become, remain, stay

19. (a) action
    (b) linking

20. intransitive

21. transitive

22. The, salty, stale, potato, the, hungry

23. We find coast redwoods only between southern Oregon and central California.

24. We see giant sequoia trees only on the western slopes of the Sierra Nevada Mountains.

25. and, but, or, not, for, yet, so

26. and

27. or

28.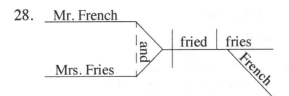

29.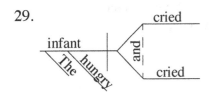

30.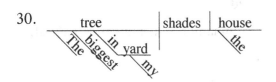

LESSON 39 Correlative Conjunctions

Practice 39

a. indict

b. indict

c. either/or

d. Neither/nor

e. Both/and

f. Not only/but also

g.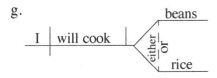

Review Set 39

1. homophones

2. too

3. among

4. biosphere

5. present

6. subject

7. exclamatory

8. car

9. ladies

10. chimneys

11. Snakes, I

12. Hey, Mom

13. The

14. Jennifer Ware

15. like

16. of the *United States

17. invented

18. have

19. does

20. was hopping

21. One, coast, ten

22. I. Television sets
    A. Screens
    B. Channels

23. I miss James R. Roe.

24. and, or, yet

25. or

26. both/and, not only/but also, neither/nor, either/or

27. Neither, nor

28. not only, but also

29. both, and

30.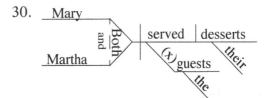

LESSON 40 The Period, Part 2: Abbreviations, Decimals

Practice 40

a. Mr. and Mrs. Pauly drove west on Sunset Blvd.

b. School begins at 8 a.m. each weekday.

c. Everybody admired Ms. Webster's Easter bonnet.

d. Our marriage ceremony was performed by Rev. John Harrison.

e. David R. Jones, Jr., plans to visit South America.

f. "Acme Toy Co." was the name printed on the box.

g. Most of us will never climb Mt. Everest.

h. Meg is sure that 7.25 (seven and twenty-five hundredths) is the answer to Prof. Wang's math problem.

i. accept

j. accept

k. except

l. accept

m. except

More Practice 40 *See answers on page 163.*

Review Set 40

1. substitute

2. triathlon

3. moral

4. dishonor

5. completed

6. have

7. shorten

8. periods

9. declarative

10. Sunday

11. halves

12. hooves or hoofs

13. Last . . . Kentridge High School . . . William Shakespeare's *Romeo and Juliet*.

14. My . . . French . . . .

15. School . . . .

16. save, since

17. of the *United States

18. of the coast *redwoods in *Montgomery State Reserve

19. Examples: clobbered, smacked, smashed, whacked

20. scratches

21. hiss

22. tapped

23. The, cinnamon-red, a, giant, a, natural, fire

24. (a) Tues.
    (b) $1.75

25. Neither/nor

26. not only/but also

27. both/and

28.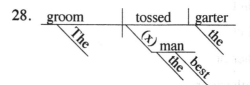

29.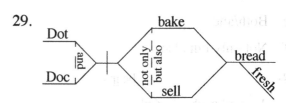

30.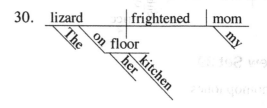

LESSON 41   **The Predicate Nominative**

Practice 41

a. maltreat

b. malnutrition

c. maladjusted

d. mal-

e. England | became \ nation

f. Queen Victoria | was \ monarch

g. queen | was \ woman

h. queen | became \ widow

Review Set 41

1. lays

2. lie

3. whose

4. who's

5. specific

6. singular

7. possessive

8. imperative

9. run-on

10. biographies

11. attorneys at law

12. The Prince of Wales, Mark Twain's *A Connecticut Yankee in King Arthur's Court.*

13. and, the, me, think, very

14. with a very small screen, TV

15. chatted

16. was

17. has discovered

18. have been learning

19. (a) intransitive
    (b) transitive

20. the, the, first, wireless, remote

21. Mrs. Henrietta B. Highbrow
    1265 S. Higginbottom Blvd.
    Uppity City, Ohio 44873

22. and, but, or, for, nor, yet, so

23. predicate

24. subject

25. TV

26. Mercury 7

27.
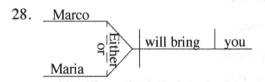

28.

29.
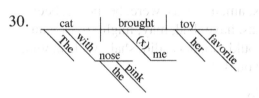

30.

LESSON 42   **Noun Case, Part 1: Nominative, Possessive**

Practice 42

a. nominative, subject

b. nominative, predicate nominative

c. possessive

d. nominative, subject

e. nominative, predicate nominative

f. sit

g. set

h. sit

i. set

Review Set 42

1. monopoly

2. punctual

3. willpower

4. Its

5. indefinite

6. conjunction

7. interrogative

8. clause

9. month

10. holiday

11. courses

12. capfuls

13. A, Fido, Danbury Street, Portland, Oregon

14. persevere, unicycle, submarine, prodigious, fewer

15. is, am, are, was, were, be, being, been, has, have, had, may, might, must, can, could, do, does, did, shall, will, should, would

16. do

17. had existed

18. had been expanding

19. deserts

20. desert

21. a.m., p.m.

22. desert

23. orthodontist

24. nominative

25. case

26. nominative

27. possessive

28.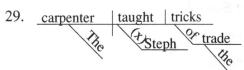
Dr. Bryce | has become \ orthodontist / an

29. carpenter | taught | tricks / The / (x)Steph / of trade / the

30.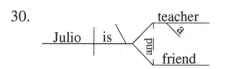
Julio | is \ teacher / a / and / friend

LESSON 43   Noun Case, Part 2: Objective

Practice 43

a. O.P.

b. I. O.

c. D.O.

d. O.P.

e. D. O.

f. I.O.

g. principle

h. principal

i. principle

j. principal

k. nominative case

l. objective case

m. possessive case

n. objective case

Review Set 43

1. sitting

2. Set

3. pore

4. incredible

5. proper

6. concrete

7. heating

8. exclamatory

9. phrase

10. stingrays

11. bluffs

12. These . . . I . . . William Shakespeare's
    As You Like It:
    All the world's . . .
    And all the men . . . .

13. I. The prefix *bio-*
    A. Biology
    B. Biography
    C. Biosphere

14. bicycle, subsoil, substitute, morale, become

15. pours

16. Examples: sits, lies, sleeps, reads, slouches, relaxes, waits

17. <u>have</u> made

18. <u>shall have</u> discovered

19. <u>will have been</u> growing

20. girlfriend

21. The, a, an, a

22. conjunction

23. objective

24. and

25. problem

26. direct object

27. object of a preposition

28. indirect object

29.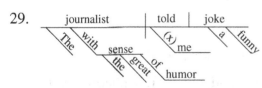

30.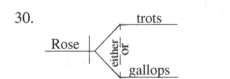

LESSON 44   The Predicate Adjective

Practice 44

a. India | was \ special

b. temples and art | were \ magnificent

c. West India Co. | became \ greedy and dishonest cruel

d. soldiers | were \ brutal

e. ultra-

f. ultraviolet

g. Ultramodern

h. ultraconservative

Review Set 44

1. maltreat

2. maladjusted

3. indicted

4. prudence

5. subject

6. abstract

7. plural

8. cried

9. shall

10. subject

11. linking

12. declarative

13. moose

14. radios

15. Informing, You

16. Hey, Mr. Wilson, English

17. tricycle, bilingual, its, too, whose

18. buzzes

19. are discussing

20. teach, skate, skip, swing, cook

21. This

22. many

23. exhausted

24. predicate

25. Correlative

26. nominative

27. objective

28.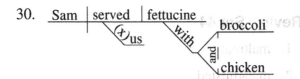

The dog grew lonely bored

29. Fresh flowers smell delightful

30. Sam served (x) us fettucine with broccoli and chicken

LESSON 45   Comparison Adjectives

Practice 45

a. flatter, comparative

b. youngest, superlative

c. most, superlative

d. hungrier, comparative

e. cutest, superlative

f. faster, comparative

g. higher, highest

h. more (or less) talkative
   most (or least) talkative

i. advise

j. advice

k. advice

l. advise

Review Set 45

1. accept

2. except

3. malnutrition

4. There

5. predicate

6. collective

7. compound

8. are

9. (has) smoked

10. complete sentence

11. cactuses or cacti

12. mosquitoes or mosquitos

13. Grandma, Grandpa Curtis, Dad

14. The

15. between *Gertrude and *Ophelia

16. hits

17. was studying

18. was

19. first

20. linking

21. comparative

22. largest

23. greater

24. Be here at 8 a.m. sharp.

25. both/and, either/or, neither/nor, not only/but also

26. Creoles

27. nominative case, predicate nominatives

28. objective case, object of a preposition

29.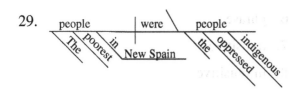

30.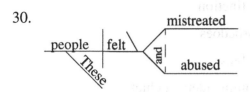

LESSON 46   Irregular Comparison Adjectives

Practice 46

a. Many

b. much

c. worst

d. More

e. Little

f. more timid

g. raise

h. raze

i. rays

More Practice 46

1. Less

2. better

3. worst

4. better

5. more reliable

6. more

7. most clever

8. braver

Review Set 46

1. malnutrition

2. set

3. dialogue

4. effect

5. interrogative

6. patted

7. are

8. superlative

9. positive

10. comparative

11. complete sentence

12. phrase

13. squid

14. ostriches

15. elephants

16. studios

17. The . . . , "The . . . ."

18. of fifteen *feet

19. of an *ostrich

20. have counted

21. will be using

22. is, am, are, was, were, be, being, been, look, feel, taste, smell, sound, seem, appear, grow, become, remain, stay

23. newer, newest

24. more intelligent, most intelligent

25. littler, littlest

26. and, but, or, for, nor, yet, so

27. John C. Fremont explored many parts of the U.S.

28. nominative

29.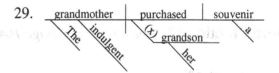

30.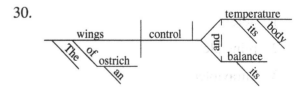

LESSON 47   The Comma, Part 1: Dates, Addresses, Series

Practice 47

a. brake

b. break

c. break

d. brake

e. Flying 670 miles per hour, American test pilot Charles Yeager broke the sound barrier on October 14, 1947.

f. The news spread in January 1849 that gold had been discovered in America. [no commas needed]

g. Christmas fell on Monday, December 25, in the year 2000.

h. The doctor moved his office to 1712 W. Duarte Road, Arcadia, California 91007.

i. Rome, Italy, attracts many tourists each year.

j. Are your friends going to Salem, Massachusetts, or Salem, Oregon?

k. The eight parts of speech include nouns, pronouns, verbs, adverbs, adjectives, prepositions, conjunctions, and interjections.

l. I have a sweet gum tree, two spruce trees, two lilac bushes, and several junipers in my front yard.

m. Siti wants to visit Tibet, Mongolia, and Indonesia.

More Practice 47   *See answers on page 164.*

Review Set 47

1. hole

2. principle

3. ultraviolet

4. fewer

5. declarative

6. phrase

7. transitive

8. intransitive

9. extinction

10. torpedoes

11. babies

12. commanders in chief

13. I.   Saving the . . .
    A. Black rats . . .
    B. The tiny . . .

14. to black *rats
in the *cliffs and *grottoes
of *Anacapa Island

15. For the murrelets' *survival
on the *island

16. is, am, are, was, were, be, being, been, has, have, had, may, might, must, can, could, do, does, did, shall, will, should, would

17. (a)   has
    (b)   have
    (c)   Have

18. had joined

19. have been observing

20. action

21. The, endangered, the

22. One hundred, this

23. both/and, either/or, not only/but also, neither/nor

24. I.   Polar bears
    A. Weight
    B. Length

25. On Wednesday, July 4, 2001, the United States celebrated Independence Day with barbecues, fireworks, and parades.

26. Please return this lost dog to 321 Beagle Ave., Roverton, Connecticut.

27. nominative

28. objective

29.

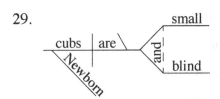

30.

```
    bears │ risk │ extinction
      \
       Polar
```

LESSON 48   Appositives

Practice 48

a. may

b. can

c. Can

d. May

e. may

f. Can

g. a popular Thanksgiving dessert

h. cinnamon

i.
```
Joe Lu (class president) │ writes │ novels
                                        \
                                         mystery
```

j. Example: Mrs. Smith, my teacher, wants me to succeed.

k. Example: Mr. Dunn, principal of Gidley School, encourages students to try hard.

More Practice 48   *See "Silly Story #3" on pages 165–166. Answers will vary.*

Review Set 48

1. prodigious

2. advice

3. accept

4. injustice

5. exclamatory

6. intransitive

7. appositive

8. Answers will vary. Example: Shirley Temple, a very famous child actress, was also called "The Little Princess."

9. Shirley Temple

10. bluffs

11. Wednesdays

12. At, Shirley Temple

13. Stand, Up, Cheer, I, Baby, Take, Bow

14. The Little Colonel, Civil War, Shirley Temple, Bill "Bojangles" Robinson

15. After her film *contract
    in short *films
    of adult *movies

16. During *1934
    in seven short *films

17. (a) am
    (b) is
    (c) are

18. had become

19. shall have watched

20. had been looking

21. is dancing, danced, has danced

22. Shirley Temple

23. bright, cheery

24. both/and

25. On Sunday, June 1, 2002, we were asked to send a copy of the *St. Louis Post-Dispatch* to 32 Marshall Blvd., Green City, Alaska.

26. Shirley Temple, dog (Rin Tin Tin is an appositive.)

27. objective case

28. a Shirley Temple fan

29. Gertrude Temple

30.
```
friend (Patricia Cheung) │ traveled
      \                        \
       My                       to China
```

LESSON 49 — The Comma, Part 2: Direct Address, Appositives, Academic Degrees

Practice 49

a. Peter, we learned about negative integers yesterday.

b. How long, good friends, must we wait before lunch?

c. Charles Dickens, author of *Oliver Twist,* wrote several notable literary works.

d. The artist Claude Monet painted a peaceful water scene by using a special method of brushing. [no commas needed]

e. Patti Anderson, R.N., applied to be a school nurse instead of a hospital nurse.

f. My dog's health is very important to Don Russell, D.V.M.

g. peace

h. piece

i. peace

j. piece

More Practice 49 *See answers on page 167.*

Review Set 49

1. respectful
2. course
3. too
4. discipline
5. imperative
6. empties
7. shall
8. dancing
9. transitive
10. articles
11. Mexico
12. Marxism
13. cantaloupe
14. children
15. Grandma Lillian
16. Hey, Grandpa
17. I, Spanish
18. for young *children and the *elderly
19. through the cantaloupe's *rind to the *fruit
20. will have tainted
21. will have been preparing
22. superlative
23. stormier, stormiest
24. On Thursday, February 14, 2002, my brother and his fiancée became Mr. and Mrs. Rodríguez.
25. "Thank you, Joyce, for the delicious meal," commented Van, the polite boyfriend of Jan.
26. Kenneth Hopkins, Ph.D., authored several books on psychology while teaching at the University of Boulder.
27. possessive case
28. Jenny's best friend
29. Dr. Flealess, a veterinarian, prescribes treatment for fleas and ticks. [Answers may vary.]
30.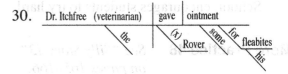

LESSON 50 — Overused Adjectives • Unnecessary Articles

Practice 50

Answers a–d will vary.

a. terrifying, scary, worrisome

b. interesting, thoughtful, entertaining

c. pleasant, fun, happy, satisfying

d. bitter, rotten, stale, disgusting, foul

e. That sort of test makes me nervous.

f. The toddlers were tired, so we put both of them to bed.

g. right

h. write

i. rite

j. wright

Review Set 50

1. Their

2. prudence

3. morale

4. consideration

5. brush

6. does

7. danced

8. demonstrative

9. possessive

10. indefinite

11. fragment

12. Indian Ocean

13. multitude

14. Earth's

15. lives

16. Along, West Coast

17. One, Christian, Easter

18. Dear Sierra Club
    Sadly . . . Can . . . ?
    Sincerely,
    An . . .

19. of *mussels
    in the *tidepools

20. throughout the *Pacific Ocean
    since the late *1970s

21. are warning

22. intransitive

23. lovelier, loveliest

24. flamboyant

25. Please give both of them directions to the sports arena.

26. Chandler, please show me that you are reliable.

27. objective case

28. *Mary Poppins*
    a talented vocalist

29. Example: Rin Tin Tin, a famous dog, captured the hearts of the American people during the Depression. [Answers may vary.]

30.
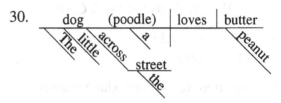

LESSON 51   **Pronouns and Antecedents**

Practice 51

a. James

b. Jenny

c. Natalie, Nicholas [for *they*];
    bikes [for *them*]

d. jacket

e. While Ellen and Tracy were waiting, Ellen completed her math assignment.

f. The primer dated back to colonial times

g. fractious

h. fraction

i. fracture

Review Set 51

1. raise

2. brake

3. may

4. piece

5. comparative

6. objective

7. direct

8. appositive

9. commas

10. were

11. interrogative

12. The, Lewis, Clark, Mississippi River, United States, America

13. I. Book list
       A. *The Indian in the Cupboard*
       B. *The House at Pooh Corner*

14. Despite the *rain
    at the *beach

15. (is) snipping, snipped, (has) snipped

16. Asian, African

17. Example: friendly, cheerful, funny, warm, jovial, sweet

18. The three planets closest to our sun are Mercury, Venus, and Earth.

19. neither/nor

20. Mars

21. Example: The nearest planet to the sun, Mercury, orbits the sun in about eighty-eight Earth days. [Answers will vary.]

22. pronoun

23. antecedent

24. before

25. go

26. before

27. it

28.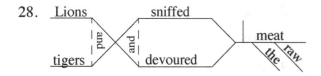

29.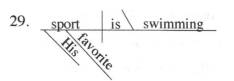

30.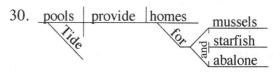

LESSON 52   The Comma, Part 3: Greetings and Closings, Last Name First

Practice 52

a. Dear Rosie,
   Thank you for arranging my student list in alphabetical order. I can see that the first name on the list is "Adams, Laurie."
   Gratefully,
   Suzanne

b. The index lists "Poe, Edgar A." as the author of "The Raven."

c. hangars

d. hangers

e. hangar

f. hangers

More Practice 52   *See answers on page 168.*

Review Set 52

1. right

2. advised

3. sympathy

4. biography

5. have

6. superlative

7. comma

8. predicate nominative

9. indirect

10. transitive

11. audience

12. Dr., Mrs. Robert Turner; Mom, English

13. with suckers; arms

14. husband and wife

15. Wendy's, bridal, tiny, pink, some, mint, three, enormous, white, a, long, silk

16. I had never seen that kind of bouquet before.

17. closing

18. comma

19. object

20. noun

21. antecedent

22. Dear Sunny,
    Your appointment is at 9 a.m.
    Sincerely,
    Bala

23. Ray Bradbury

24. Fahrenheit 451

25. One of my favorite books, *To Kill a Mockingbird,* isn't about killing birds.

26. she/Annabel

27. will have marched

28. have given

29.
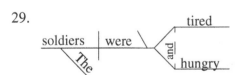

30.
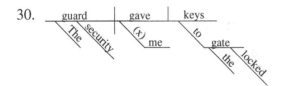

LESSON 53 Personal Pronouns

Practice 53

a. verb

b. less

c. me, first person

d. she, third person

e. you, second person

f. us, plural

g. me, singular

h. subject

i. direct object

j. indirect object

k. possession

More Practice 53

1. we, first person plural;
   you, second person singular or plural

2. they, third person plural

3. him, third person singular

4. They, third person plural;
   their, third person plural;
   it, third person singular

5. you, second person singular or plural;
   my, first person singular

6. her, third person singular

7. We, first person plural;
   our, first person plural;
   them, third person plural

8. I, first person singular;
   them, third person plural

9. They, third person plural;
   my, first person singular

10. She, third person singular;
    us, first person plural

11. we, subject;
    you, object

12. they, subject

13. him, object

14. they, subject;
    their, possessive;
    it, object

15. you, subject;
    my, possessive

16. her, object

17. we, subject;
    our, possessive;
    them, object

18. I, subject;
    them, object

19. they, subject;
    my, possessive

20. she, subject;
    us, object

Review Set 53

1. They're

2. except

3. ultramodern

4. incredible

5. continuing

6. positive

7. people

8. first

9. second

10. third

11. run-on

12. buck

13. The, Amish, East

14. hurried, flocked

15. the

16. larger, largest

17. Read Henry W. Longfellow's "The Psalm of Life" by tomorrow.

18. "Zorilla, Britnii" was the last name on the list.

19. The last entry in the encyclopedia was "Zweig, Arnold."

20. Dear Isabel,
    Please use these boxes, racks, and hangers for your clothes.
    Love,
    Mom

21. Thomas Gillespie, the president of Princeton Seminary, preached about God's justice and mercy.

22. (mother,) *diamond

23. owner

24. transitive

25. object of a preposition

26. a young Englishman

27. South Africa

28. Cecil Rhodes, a man with great ambition, went into politics.

29. his/Cecil Rhodes

30.

LESSON 54   Irregular Verbs, Part 2

Practice 54

a. continual

b. continuous

c. continuous

d. continual

e. knew

f. sworn

g. sunk

h. frozen

i. worn

j. swore

k. grown

l. shrank

m. blew, blown

n. knew, known

o. threw, thrown

p. grew, grown

q. bore, borne

r. tore, torn

s. wore, worn

t. swore, sworn

u. began, begun

v. rang, rung

w. sang, sung

x. drank, drunk

y. chose, chosen

z. spoke, spoken

Review Set 54

1. pores

2. principal

3. ores

4. whole

5. Conjunctions

[Note on 6 and 7: *You* and *yours* can be either singular or plural.)

6. singular

7. plural

8. case

9. objects

10. Example: I placed the coat on the hanger.

11. peonies

12. linking

13. action

14. Dear Father-in-law Jeremy
Thirty-five, It
Gratefully
Son-in-law Francis

15. (a) froze, frozen
(b) broke, broken
(c) stole, stolen

16. known

17. grew

18. torn

19. sung

20. (a) more loyal, most loyal
(b) happier, happiest

21. The abbreviations for the days of the week are Sun., Mon., Tue., Wed., Thurs., Fri., and Sat.

22. nominative

23. predicate

24. direct object

25. a 10,457-foot volcano

26. an American Indian group

27. Lassen Peak, a volcano in Northern California, erupted from 1914 to 1921.

28. object

29.

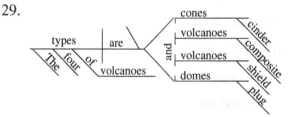

30.

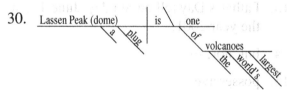

LESSON 55   Nominative Pronoun Case

Practice 55

a. *Refer to the chart in Example 1.*

b. They are faithful friends.

c. The best writer was she.

d. invalid

e. invalid

f. She and I will come.

g. I, she, they, he, we

h. he

i. she

j. he

k. I

Review Set 55

1. effect

2. diameter

3. discretion

4. fainted

5. clause

6. possessive

7. geese

8. into their *bodies,
   through a *funnel,
   like *missiles,
   through the *ocean

9. <u>can</u> escape

10. wore, worn

11. worse, worst

12. more, most

13. Father's Day fell on Sunday, June 17, in the year 2001.

14. but, nor, so

15. possessive

16. nominative

17. indirect object

18. brown and red

19. an easy catch

20. Example: My birthday is in July, the hottest month of the year.

21. her/Winnie

22. mine, first person singular

23. they, third person plural

24. You, second person singular or plural

25. *Refer to the chart in Example 1.*

26. It belongs to Henrietta.

27. The winner of the race was you.

28. b

29. you

30.

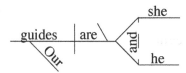

LESSON 56   **The Comma, Part 4: Introductory and Interrupting Elements, Afterthoughts, Clarity**

Practice 56

a. Yes, I've heard that the Arabian camel can go without water for over two weeks.

b. Of course, a horse cannot do that.

c. The jackrabbit, I believe, cools itself on the hot deserts through his tall, thin ears.

d. The camel, it is said, is a difficult animal to ride.

e. Of all the ideas, rafting the river was our favorite.

f. When we were through, the glass door sparkled.

g. you're

h. your

i. You're

j. your

k. You're

More Practice 56   *See answers on page 169.*

Review Set 56

1. peace
2. wright
3. fractious
4. Can
5. less
6. do
7. possessive
8. nouns
9. jack-o'-lanterns
10. declarative
11. The Cabreras and I visited Hoover Dam and Lake Mead on our visit to Nevada.
12. William Shakespeare . . . *King Lear:*
   Men must endure
   Their going hence, even as their coming hither.
   Ripeness is all.
13. *Refer to the chart in Lesson 17.*
14. No, new, oppressive
15. intransitive
16. transitive
17. and, but, or, for, nor, yet, so
18. neither/nor
19. nominative case, subject
20. possessive case
21. nominative case, predicate nominative
22. Ayeesha's address is 327 W. Longden Ave., Eureka, Kansas.
23. a military dictator
24. pronoun
25. nominative, objective
26. I, she, they, he, we
27. The bus driver waited for me.
28. nominative case
29. objective case
30.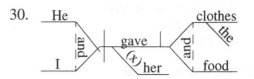

LESSON 57   Objective Pronoun Case

Practice 57

a. *Refer to the chart in Example 1.*
b. The wind blew her down.
c. John sang me a lullaby.
d. He has sung to us. *[Also correct: To us he has sung.]*
e. lend
f. borrow
g. borrow
h. lend
i. Don't overlook him or me.
j. me, him, them, her, us
k. him
l. him
m. me

Review Set 57

1. *Refer to the chart from Lesson 55.*
2. *Refer to the chart in Example 1 of this lesson.*
3. invalid
4. depreciates
5. direct
6. coordinating conjunction
7. you're
8. Your
9. played
10. charisma

11. I. William Shakespeare
    A. *King Lear*
    B. *The Merchant of Venice*

12. into, of, on, out, round

13. This

14. good—soothing, magnificent, melodic, splendid, tuneful, etc.

15. charm, (is) charming, charmed, (has) charmed

16. Eurydice

17. objective, possessive

18. objective

19. antecedent

20. nominative

21. object of a preposition

22. indirect object

23. direct object

24. she

25. The caterer sent them a menu.

26. nominative case

27. the three-headed watchdog of the underworld

28.
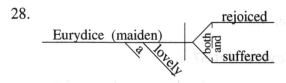

29.
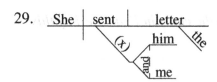

30.
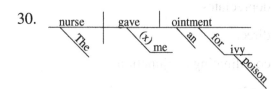

LESSON 58   **Personal Pronoun Case Forms**

Practice 58

a. objective case

b. nominative case

c. possessive case

d. object of preposition

e. subject

f. direct object

g. indirect object

h. possession

i. they

j. me

k. rise

l. raise

m. raise

n. rise

Review Set 58

1. reliable

2. same

3. waste

4. coarse

5. indirect

6. taller

7. worn

8. fragment

9. man's

10. Annette, Grandpa

11. object

12. case

13. objective

14. Greek

15. repeated

16. will have been punishing

17. and

18. possessive case

19. nominative case

20. objective case

21. Apollo, Daphne, Orpheus, Eurydice, Echo, and Narcissus are all characters from Greek myths.

22. Dear Adrienne,
School will begin on September 9, 2001.
Your friend,
Michelle

23. supervisor

24. Marta

25. *Refer to the chart in Lesson 55.*

26. My brother rescued me.

27. nominative

28. objective

29.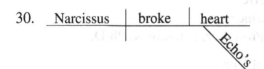

30.

LESSON 59 — Diagramming Pronouns

Practice 59

a.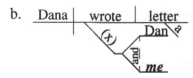

b.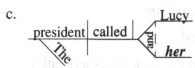

c.

d. sibling

e. devise

f. devise

g. sibling(s)

Review Set 59

1. integrity

2. persevere

3. Whose

4. between

5. faster

6. hottest

7. replies

8. Once there lived a sculptor named Pygmalion. He made statues of the finest design.

9. stingrays

10. I, Spanish-speaking, North, I, West

11. at his *art

12. content, happy

13. had loved

14. Pygmalion

15. conjunctions

16. nominative

17. Personal

18. Look under "London, Jack" in the catalog to find *The Call of the Wild.*

19. Hey, Pop, have you ever read about Pygmalion, a famous sculptor?

20. Dr. U. R. Fine, I think, practices in Omaha.

21. Yes, Pygmalion died a happy man.

22. After studying, the students practice basketball, soccer, and volleyball.

23. b

24. *Refer to the chart in Lesson 57.*

25. me

26. indirect object

27. predicate nominative

28. subject

29.

30.

LESSON 60   Possessive Pronouns and Possessive Adjectives

Practice 60

a. its

b. their

c. their

d. your

e. ours

f. leave

g. let

h. leave

i. let

More Practice 60

1. their

2. They're

3. its

4. ours

5. hers

6. yours

7. your

8. its

9. It's, its

10. Your, ours

11. Their

12. They're

1. two

2. less

3. monorails

4. postscript

5. periods

6. First

7. Second

8. Third

9. second

10. first

11. third

12. he

13. hers

14. Yours

15. sheep

16. Dear Mieko,
   An, One, Japanese, Christianity, Japan,
   Are
   Sincerely,
   Professor, Knowings, Ph.D.

17. of Venus

18. is, am, are, was, were, be, being, been,
   has, have, had, may, might, must, can,
   could, do, does, did, shall, will, should,
   would

19. became

20. imperative, declarative

21. neither/nor,
   either/or,
   not only/but also,
   both/and

22. nominative

23. her, third person

24. We, plural

25. She wore the same dress as Caitlin.

26. b

27. him, us

28. my, your, his, her, its, their, mine

29.
```
 Venus | was \ jealous
                \ of
                   Psyche
```

30.
```
 They | had mailed | invitation
           \(x)      \ an
             him
```

LESSON 61   Dependent and Independent Clauses • Subordinating Conjunctions

Practice 61

a. dependent

b. independent

c. independent

d. dependent

e. Unless

f. even though

g. When

h. Polychromatic

i. color

j. many

k. many

l. syllables

More Practice 61   *See answers on page 170.*

Review Set 61

1. Your

2. lend

3. rise

4. devise

5. wishes

6. swore

7. pronouns

8. transitive

9. possessive

10. imperative

11. clause

12. after, although, as, as if, as soon as, as though

13. if

14. Japan

15. Wiltshire, Yorkshire, Oxfordshire, Cornwall, England

16. will have covered

17. by the *emperor in *1868

18. forty-five

19. The Japanese liked that kind of emperor.

20. Meiji ruled wisely. His first concern was to unite the country.

21. both/and,
    neither/nor,
    either/or,
    not only/but also

22. nominative case

23. On July 28, 2001, a big event occurred at 323 March Street, Bridle City, Iowa.

24. *Refer to the chart in Lesson 55.*

25. object of a preposition

26. objective case

27. nominative case

28.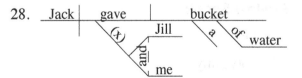

29.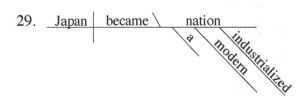

30.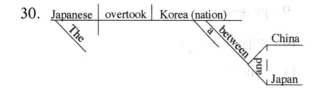

LESSON 62   Reflexive and Intensive Pronouns

Practice 62

a. I

b. ourselves

c. You

d. themselves

e. teach

f. teach

g. learn

h. learn, teach

More Practice 62

1. himself

2. themselves

3. themselves

4. I

5. me

6. themselves

7. himself

8. themselves

9. himself

10. he

Review Set 62

1. Leave

2. polygamy

3. break

4. Can

5. born

6. sung

7. possessive

8. Reflexive

9. Since

10. unless

11. because, before, even though, if, in order that

12. cupcake

13. I. Voices
    A. Soprano
    B. Alto
    C. Tenor
    D. Bass

14. <u>can</u> categorize

15. have been entertaining

16. During middle school *years

17. Austrian

18. Dr. Wayne Crabb, the choral director at St. John's School, scheduled the concert for Friday, Dec. 10.

19. me

20. nominative

21. possessive case

22. Mr. Yamashita, the art teacher, submitted pictures, poems, and other items of interest to the yearbook committee.

23. transitive

24. intransitive

25. b

26. indirect objects

27. possessive case

28.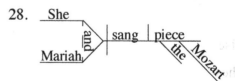

29.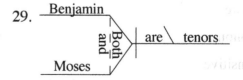

30.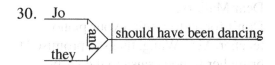
Jo
and
they
| should have been dancing

LESSON 63   **The Comma, Part 5:**
            Descriptive Adjectives,
            Dependent Clauses

Practice 63

a. London often finds itself in deep, dense
    fog.

b. I brought my biggest, warmest coat to the
    campout, but all I really needed was my
    blue cotton jacket.

c. When you go to the store, get a few
    tomatoes.

d. If they look mushy, buy some cantaloupe
    instead.

e. As soon as you get home, we'll make a
    huge salad.

f. dessert

g. desert

h. desert

i. dessert

More Practice 63   *See answers on page 171.*

Review Set 63

1. teaches

2. invalid

3. continual

4. hangers

5. dependent

6. bosses

7. spoke

8. blew

9. stole

10. false

11. ourselves

12. complete

13. since, so that, than, that, though

14. dependent

15. and, but, or, nor, for, yet, so

16. calendar

17. Grandma and Grandpa Angles grew up
    in Scotland.

18. sounds

19. action verb

20. linking verb

21. in some *poems

22. couplet

23. Mr. Atwater, please introduce us to that
    tall, mysterious gentleman in gray.

24. Stanzas give a poem a distinct,
    interesting look.

25. antecedent

26. We, first person

27. She fed her faithful dog.

28. it, direct object

29. It, nominative case

30.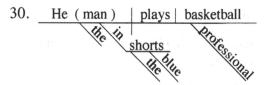
He (man) | plays | basketball
the in shorts professional
the blue

LESSON 64   **Compound Sentences •**
            Coordinating Conjunctions

Practice 64

a. simple

b. compound; and

c. compound; and, but

d. simple

e. compound; or

f.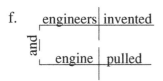

g. fore

h. four

i. for

j. fore

Review Set 64

1. fraction

2. substitute

3. lie

4. Fewer

5. independent

6. compound

7. thought

8. coordinating

9. are

10. were

11. began

12. grew

13. yours

14. himself

15. Example: He played in the school band concert.

16. unless, until, when, whenever, where, wherever, while

17. independent

18. and, but, or, nor, for, yet, so

19. wives

20. Georgia, Louisiana, and Florida are located in the South.

21. "of American civilization" modifies "story"

    "in the twentieth century" modifies "civilization"

22. Dear Mallory,
    Don't forget to remind your piano teacher, Mrs. Wang, that she promised to bring her famous salsa to the party. Unless I'm mistaken, everyone will want the recipe.
    Gratefully,
    Heather

23. While I see your point, I don't agree with you.

24. b

25. The best high jumper was she.

26. them, plural

27. me, us, you, him, her, it, them

28. her, direct object

29.

and	system	made
	travel	provided

30.

but	people	supported
	people	disliked

LESSON 65 **The Comma, Part 6: Compound Sentences, Direct Quotations**

Practice 65

a. and, but, or, nor, for, yet, so

b. for

c. yet

d. but

e. Romeo drank the poison, and he kissed Juliet for the last time.

f. Juliet slept peacefully through Romeo's kiss, and she awoke to find him dead.

g. Marcella said, "I've always wanted to fly an airplane."

h. "I like to get the big picture," she explained.

i. antiseptics

j. antiseptic

k. against

l. antisocial

m. antisocial

More Practice 65 *See answers on page 172.*

Review Set 65

1. conscience

2. poor

3. sowing

4. principal

5. predicate

6. more

7. chose

8. wore

9. known

10. they

11. Your

12. themselves

13. (a) dependent
    (b) independent
    (c) dependent

14. when

15. (a) intransitive
    (b) transitive

16. The, Chinese

17. Transvaal

18. indirect object

19. direct object

20. object of a preposition

21. Rhodes was severely criticized for attacking the Boers, and he was asked to step down as prime minister.

22. Mr. Lancaster explained, "The Boers were ready for the British to attack again."

23. people

24. objective

25. I, she, they, he, we

26. *Refer to the chart in Lesson 57.*

27.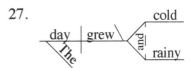

28.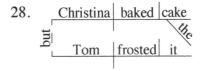

29.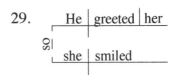

30.

LESSON 66   **Relative Pronouns**

Practice 66

a. who

b. who

c. whomever

d. that

e. whom

f.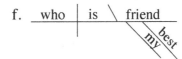

g. dilemma

h. dilemma

More Practice 66

1. who

2. who

3. whom

4. whom

5. whom

6. who

7. who

8. who

Review Set 66

1. polygon

2. let

3. siblings

4. raised

5. shall

6. first

7. second

8. third

9. who

10. who

11. whom

12. she

13. himself

14. people, animals

15. exclamatory

16. is

17. Would, African, Siberian, Canada

18. in the Komodo's *mouth

19. Indonesian, Komodo

20. The last three months of the year are abbreviated Oct., Nov., and Dec.

21. Although

22. possessive case

23. As for me, I'm going to plant geraniums, not petunias, this spring.

24. antecedent

25. b

26. objective case

27. myself, yourself, himself, herself, itself

28. ourselves, yourselves, themselves

29. who, whom, whose, what, which, that

30.

LESSON 67   Pronoun Usage

Practice 67

a. We

b. us

c. us

d. I

e. we

f. hemi-

g. hemiplegia

h. hemistich

i. hemispheres

More Practice 67

1. he

2. We

3. us

4. she

5. him

6. she

7. he

8. they

9. We

10. us

Review Set 67

1. fracture

2. write

3. rays

4. advice

5. did

6. antecedent

7. themselves

8. intensive

9. nouns

10. apposition

11. cats

12. phrase

13. Along, India, Southeast Asia

14. Oh, Cousin Katrina, English

15. of wild *cats

16. Ms. LeAnn J. Baker, Ph.D.
    2700 W. Jenkins Ave.
    St. Paul, Minnesota

17. compound, so

18. objects of a preposition (with)

19. Janine's favorite dog is a large, quiet black poodle.

20. he brushed his teeth

21. <u>After</u> he ate breakfast

22. We, first

23. she, third

24. Any six of the following: yours, he, him, his, she, her, hers, it, I, me, mine, you, its

25. Any six of the following: we, us, yours, you, they, them, theirs

26. ours, yours, hers

27. nominative case

28.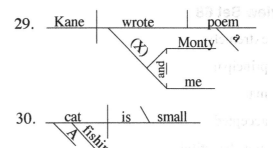

29.

30.

LESSON 68 — Interrogative Pronouns

Practice 68

a. what

b. none (*which* is an adjective)

c. Whose

d. Whom

e. Whose

f. Who

g. interrogative pronoun

h. adjective

i. hear

j. hear

k. Here

l. here

More Practice 68

1. Who's

2. Whose

3. Who

4. whom

5. Whom

6. Who's

7. Whose

8. whom

9. Who

10. Whom

Grammar and Writing 6   **61**   **Teacher Guide**
Student Edition Answers

Review Set 68

1. extremely

2. principal

3. mal-

4. accepted

5. most beautiful

6. case

7. possessive

8. possessive

9. Possessive pronouns

10. Their

11. himself

12. interrogative

13. run-on

14. intransitive

15. transitive

16. community

17. Wolfgang Mozart, my favorite composer, was born in Salzburg, Austria.

18. in runoff *water

19. and, but, or, nor, for, yet, so

20. On Friday, June 15, 2001, the Los Angeles Lakers defeated the Philadelphia Seventy-Sixers to capture their second consecutive NBA Championship.

21. The oceanographer explained, "The way that plants and animals live together in a wetland community helps slow the flow of runoff water, and this keeps the coastal waters from being flooded with dirt."

22. plural

23. singular

24. objective case

25. nominative case

26. Grandma did not swim today

27. <u>Although</u> she enjoys the ocean

28. who, whom, whose, what, which, that

29. who, whom, whose, what, which, whomever, whoever, whichever, whatever

30.

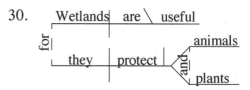

LESSON 69   Quotation Marks, Part 1

Practice 69

a. none

b. none

c. Imagine someone saying to Shaquille O'Neal, "You can't play in the National Basketball Association because you are black!"

d. "Of course," the man went on, "that's ridiculous."

e. Mr. Towner said to his class, "Jackie Robinson opened the way for players of all races to succeed in professional sports."

f. antifreeze

g. antifreeze

h. antidote

i. against

More Practice 69   *See answers on page 173.*

Review Set 69

1. indict

2. there

3. sew

4. discretion

5. four, desserts

6. dishes

7. longest

8. I

9. yourself

10. who

11. Which

12. That

13. whom

14. who

15. begins

16. (is) dripping, dripped, (has) dripped

17. My best friend, Pat Newmar, won a trip to Honolulu, Hawaii.

18. Belva Lockwood

19. her, me, him, them, us

20. he read a whole novel

21. <u>While</u> he was waiting for the doctor

22. mine, yours, his, hers, ours, theirs

23. I, she, they, he, we

24. objective case

25. nominative case

26. linking verb

27. action verb

28.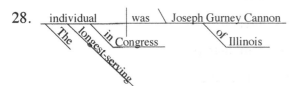

29.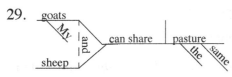

30.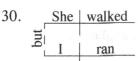

Practice 70

a. humility

b. arrogance

c. Washington Irving's short story "The Legend of Sleepy Hollow" is read by students everywhere.

d. Can you play the song "America the Beautiful" for me?

e. Mark Twain's short story "The Mysterious Stranger" is not as well known as his novel *Tom Sawyer*.

f.   "Who is your master, young man? if it be a proper question. I should judge he is a good one, from what I see."

"He is Squire Gordon, of Birtwick Park, the other side the Beacon Hills," said James.

"Ah! so, so, I have heard tell of him; fine judge of horses, ain't he? the best rider in the county."

"I believe he is," said James, "but he rides very little now, since the poor young master was killed."

More Practice 70   *See answers on pages 174–175.*

Review Set 70

1. diagonal

2. poured

3. oars

4. postwar

5. who

6. that

7. Who

8. dirties

9. Had come

10. Queen Elizabeth

11. tornadoes or tornados

12. industrious

13. either/or,
    neither/nor,
    not only/but also,
    both/and

14. Elijah, Enoch

15. Shaquille O'Neal, the Los Angeles
    Lakers' center, received the MVP trophy
    for the 2001 NBA Championship.

16. objective

17. nominative

18. b

19. Helen raced him and won.

20. Delbert made her an avocado sandwich.

21. indirect object

22. direct object

23. The fishing cat has a double layer of fur

24. <u>so that</u> it doesn't get wet all the way to
    the skin; <u>when</u> it is fishing

25. who

26. Quan said, "I once saw a twelve-foot sea
    snake curled up on the surface of the
    water."

27. "To Build a Fire," a short story written
    by Jack London, depicts the dangers of
    freezing weather.

28.

29.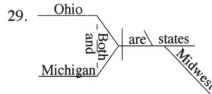

30.

LESSON 71 — Demonstrative Pronouns

Practice 71

a. semi-

b. semiconscious

c. semiprecious

d. semifinal

e. This painting

f. Those Boxers

g. This name

h. These reasons

i. This class

j. pointing

Review Set 71

1. moral

2. punctual

3. respectful

4. same

5. himself

6. clause

7. These

8. interrogative

9. demonstrative

10. imperative

11. change, match

12. had changed

13. In *The Voyage of the Beagle,* the author
    . . . color.

14. Dr. Samuel O. Mast explains . . .
    background.

15. Jahnelle and her mother serve . . . St.
    Stephen's . . . Friday nights.

16. Concerning color *changes,
    by the *expansion and *contraction,
    of the pigment *cells

17. changes

18. (a) intransitive
    (b) transitive

19. and, but, or, nor, for, yet, so

20. Dr. Mast reported, "The color adaptations in flounder probably resulted from stimuli received through the eyes."

21. Mast also shared that simple things like heat and light will cause a color change in some animals. [none needed]

22. pronoun

23. antecedent

24. nominative

25. nominative

26. objective

27. I, we, he, she, they

28. his, her, their, my

29.
They | were watching | fireworks
the / in sky / the

30.
frog | can turn \ black
A / tree

LESSON 72   Indefinite Pronouns

Practice 72

a. All, plural

b. Nobody, singular

c. is

d. are

e. is

f. has, its

g. soak, their

h. sells, it, is

i. wear

j. ware(s)

k. where

l. wear, where

More Practice 72

1. E
2. P
3. S
4. S
5. S
6. E
7. S
8. P
9. S
10. P
11. S
12. P
13. S
14. S
15. P
16. E
17. S
18. P
19. E
20. E

Additional Practice 72

See "Silly Story #4" on pages 176–177. Answers will vary.

Review Set 72

1. homonyms
2. homophones
3. waste
4. honor
5. most sensitive
6. First
7. possessive
8. who
9. which
10. that

11. him

12. near

13. indefinite

14. snakes

15. Can sting

16. denies

17. were biting

18. concrete

19. I. Occupations
    A. French teacher
    B. Biology teacher

20. over the *ground,
    with its *tongue

21. His

22. either/or,
    neither/nor,
    both/and,
    not only/but also

23. 1. Even though the people in
    Shakespeare's time believed
    2. that snakes could sting
    3. that this is a falsehood

24. we know now

25. Even though, that, that

26. me, us, him, her, them

27. Several, plural

28. his, hers

29.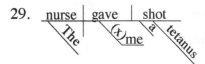

30.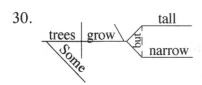

LESSON 73   Italics or Underline

Practice 73

a. stationery

b. stationary

c. National Geographic

d. is

e. eucalyptus

f. jolie

g. Pilgrim

More Practice 73   *See answers on page 178.*

Review Set 73

1. dishonor

2. earth

3. course

4. self-discipline

5. worst

6. Italics

7. Second

8. nominative

9. me

10. I

11. whom

12. we

13. who

14. far

15. fragment

16. phrase

17. look, feel, taste, sound, smell

18. Some, plural

19. Europeans, Austrian Alps

20. great; Example: exceptional

21. speller

22. *Phantom of the Opera*

23. compound

24. Howard instructed, "Today, we are going
    to learn a new song."

Tina added, "Listen to the soprano part."

25. yours, hers

26. themselves

27. few, several, ones, both, many, others

28. of humility, sense

29.

30.

LESSON 74   **Irregular Verbs, Part 3**

Practice 74

a. caught, (has) caught

b. came, (has) come

c. cost, (has) cost

d. dove or dived, (has) dived

e. dragged, (has) dragged

f. drew, (has) drawn

g. drowned, (has) drowned

h. drove, (has) driven

i. eaten

j. found

k. drove

l. cost

m. forgave

n. caught

o. flew

p. fell

q. bear

r. bear

s. bare

t. bear

More Practice 74   *See answers on pages 179–180.*

Review Set 74

1. geology

2. geography

3. biology

4. willpower

5. will

6. Third

7. me

8. I

9. whom

10. who

11. whom

12. This

13. Example: The owl is the symbol of wisdom.

14. intransitive

15. transitive

16. built, (has) built

17. authorities

18. My friend from the Midwest . . . "Howdy, Grandma, . . . Dr. Noodleman yet?"

19. us

20. We shall study owls, falcons, and hawks.

21. The owl, a bird of ill omen, represents death to the superstitious.

22. Mr. Parmenter said, "The owl can turn its head in almost a complete circle."

23. everybody, singular

24. Authorities confess

25. that owls are not the smartest of birds

26. It's

27. all, none, any, some, most

28.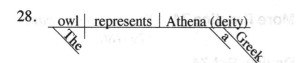

29.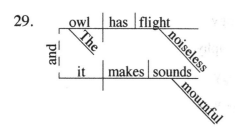

30.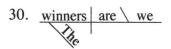

LESSON 75 Irregular Verbs, Part 4

Practice 75

a. hid, (has) hidden or hid

b. held, (has) held

c. laid, (has) laid

d. led, (has) led

e. lent, (has) lent

f. mistook, (has) mistaken

g. put, (has) put

h. sold, (has) sold

i. hid

j. held

k. laid

l. led

m. reconcile

n. reconcile

o. reconciliation

More Practice 75 *See answers on pages 181–182.*

Review Set 75

1. life

2. conscientious

3. diligent

4. biographies

5. have

6. are

7. mistook

8. him

9. ours

10. Whoever

11. whomever

12. Whom

13. Those

14. phrase

15. women

16. The

17. annoying

18. Democritus

19. Dear Democritus,
   Why are you continually smiling?
   Sincerely,
   Socrates

20. Democritus, some believe, put out his own eyes so that he might not be distracted from his thinking.

21. When she was a young child, Ruth's favorite song was "The Farmer in the Dell."

22. <u>Newsweek</u>, <u>Time</u>

23. Hugo

24. we, us, they, you, yours, them, theirs

25. nominative case

26. possessive case

27. herself

28. Much, singular

29. you | Will grow | tomatoes
(x) me some cherry

30. babysitter | hid | scissors
The the with points sharp

LESSON 76 Irregular Verbs, Part 5

Practice 76

a. took; (has) taken

b. set; (has) set

c. taught; (has) taught

d. told; (has) told

e. woke; (has) woken

f. sprang or sprung; (has) sprung

g. strove; (has) striven

h. shut; (has) shut

i. written

j. slept

k. thought

l. taught

m. told

n. woken

o. sat

p. shut

q. consequence

r. consequential

More Practice 76 *See answers on pages 183–184.*

Review Set 76

1. filled; built; boiled; scrubbed; wrung; hung

2. reconcile

3. bear

4. stationery

5. ware

6. varies

7. shrunk

8. led

9. was

10. We

11. Those

12. less

13. interrogative

14. demonstrative

15. number

16. direct

17. underlining

18. declarative

19. phrase

20. Do appear; intransitive

21. Puerto Rico, Caribbean Sea

22. I. Camels
   A. Hump
   B. Spine

23. Like the *camel,
   of *sheep,
   in their *tails

24. The, gasoline, the, one, single

25. possible

26. In 1885, a man from Munich, Germany, constructed a tricycle driven by a crude internal combustion engine.

27. In 1891, the builder of the motorized tricycle, Dr. Karl Benz, built the first gasoline-driven automobile in Germany.

28. In 1885, Gottlieb Daimler, also a German, installed a gasoline engine on a bicycle, and later he patented a high-speed internal combustion engine.

29. who, whom, whose, what, which, that.

30. carriages | were \ impractical
    Steam-driven

LESSON 77   The Exclamation Mark • The Question Mark • The Dash

Practice 77

a. Whew! That math test was really difficult!

b. Do you understand place value?

c. Who painted *The Ladies of Avignon?*

d. I know! It's Pablo Picasso!

e. It's just what I wanted—a lime green bowling ball.

f. The party starts—let's see—about eight o'clock.

g. That's all my sister dreams of—horses.

h. scent

i. sent

j. cent

k. cent

l. sent

m. scent

Review Set 77

1. semiprecious

2. antifreeze

3. against

4. Here

5. Where

6. who

7. who

8. who

9. oral

10. who

11. Those

12. she ["did" is understood]

13. indirect

14. underline

15. exclamation

16. Ferdinand Magellan

17. Did circumnavigate

18. (is) going, went, (has) gone

19. was killed, intransitive

20. Did complete, transitive

21. rumor

22. Mrs. Norris, German, Let's, English

23. around the *world
    in a single *voyage

24. and, but, or, for, nor, yet, so

25. possessive case

26. Dear Uncle Mark,
    That dirty, shaggy, yellow dog we found last Saturday is doing fine. We fed him, gave him a bath, and trimmed his fur. Now he is a clean, sleek, yellow dog.
    Happily,
    Betsy

27. crew

28. nominative, objective, possessive

29. She | was opening | umbrella
    for her
    raindrops | were falling

30. queen (Queen Anne) | bore | children
    An English   seventeen

Practice 78

a. was

b. were

c. care

d. makes

e. make

f. has

g. anxious

h. eager

i. eager

j. anxious

More Practice 78

1. sound

2. are

3. live

4. grow

5. are

6. stay

7. was

8. were

9. were

10. have

Review Set 78

1. humility

2. antiseptic

3. learn

4. Desert

5. run

6. brought

7. saw

8. shaken

9. their

10. who

11. who

12. appositive

13. nearby

14. is

15. direct

16. question

17. run-on sentence

18. Have been carrying

19. (a) antelope or antelopes
    (b) foxes
    (c) wolves

20. Milton High School's debate team meets on Thursdays.

21. in California *history

22. Spanish, California

23. nice; long, silky, wiry, handsome, thin, broken, etc.

24. cat

25. me

26. themselves

27. who

28. Leonardo da Vinci's most famous painting, the *Mona Lisa*, features a woman whose eyes seem to follow the viewer.

29.

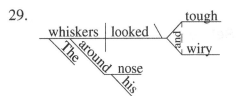

30.

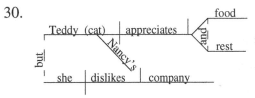

Practice 79

a. were   pictures | were

b. was   vehicle | was

c. is   choice | is

d. are   choices | are

e. was   choice | was

f. imply

g. infer

h. infer

i. imply

More Practice 79

1. sits
2. was
3. is
4. go
5. are
6. blasts
7. makes
8. were

Review Set 79

1. desert
2. hear
3. for
4. half
5. told
6. are
7. put
8. rose
9. go
10. scares
11. tastier
12. We
13. who
14. far
15. dash
16. Example: All summer long we boated on the lake
17. children
18. "of gases" modifies "release;" "in Swiss cheese" modifies "holes"
19. us
20. a cheese from Oregon
21. Well, the distinct, pungent odor of Swiss cheese proves distasteful to some.
22. I
23. whoever, whosoever, whomever, whichever, whatever
24. several, both, few, many, others
25. Indirect quotation; no quotation marks needed
26. One of the organist's favorite songs is "It Is Well with My Soul."
27. <u>My Fair Lady</u>
28. (is) sleeping, slept, (has) slept
29.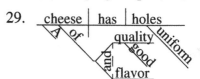
30.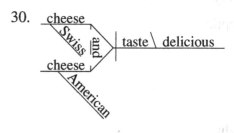

LESSON 80 Subject-Verb Agreement, Part 3

Practice 80

a. aren't

b. is

c. weren't

d. There are

e. has

f. suburb

g. icon

h. suburbs

More Practice 80

1. is

2. is

3. needs

4. wants

5. is

6. knows

7. remembers

8. sees

9. was

10. were

11. isn't

12. doesn't

13. don't

14. aren't

15. aren't

Review Set 80

1. is

2. was

3. was

4. deserves

5. knows

6. aren't

7. isn't

8. There are

9. mistaken

10. seen

11. best

12. me

13. emphasis

14. scent

15. semiconscious

16. consequences

17. malnutrition

18. has called

19. had been living

20. I, *Flowery Kingdom*

21. Many

22. fangs

23. Neither/nor

24. A large, rounded mass of gold in its original state is called a nugget

25. The largest gold nugget was found in Victoria, Australia, on February 5, 1989.

26. Holterman bragged, "I extracted the biggest nugget."

27. Emily said, "I don't want to do the dishes tonight, Mom."

    "I know you don't, Emily, but it is your turn," Mom insisted.

    "But I have loads of homework!" cried Emily.

    Mom pointed out, "Then you should have watched less television this afternoon."

28. merci beaucoup

29.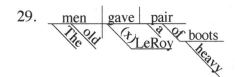

30. Flowery Kingdom | is \ name — for China
    an \ ancient

LESSON 81   Subject-Verb Agreement, Part 4

Practice 81

a. was

b. was

c. has

d. was

e. allegiance

f. allegation

g. allege

Review Set 81

1. icon

2. suburb

3. inferred

4. anxiety

5. held

6. is

7. pronouns

8. Direct

9. they

10. indirect

11. I

12. interrogative

13. could have been

14. will have been studying

15. (a) handfuls
    (b) scarves
    (c) oxen

16. The first shot of World War I, I am told, was in June of 1914.

17. The high school has a chess club, so why doesn't it have a checkers club?

18. I. World War I
    A. Countries involved
    B. Important dates

19. Franklin

20. Not only/but also

21. the students didn't want the fascinating lecture to end

22. Even though they were tired

23. Even though

24. me

25. other, one, nobody, anybody, much

26. James answered, "Yes, Rob and they will be here soon."

27. "Each spring," Wes explained, "the swallows return to Capistrano."

28. underline

29. exclamation point

30.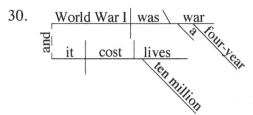

LESSON 82   Negatives • Double Negatives

Practice 82

a. had

b. could

c. anything

d. ever

e. ever

f. vain

g. vane

h. vain

i. vein

j. vein

More Practice 82

1. any, any

2. any

3. anybody

4. either

5. anyone

6. anywhere

7. any

8. ever

9. any

10. anything

Review Set 82

1. cent

2. sent

3. consequential

4. stationary

5. Its

6. Demonstrative

7. paragraph

8. quotation

9. underline

10. interrogative

11. no

12. elements

13. would cost

14. in the human body

15. body

16. elements

17. chemical, human

18. one

19. statue

20. *The Thinker*

21.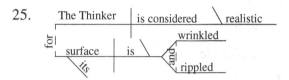

22. *The Thinker* is considered realistic

23. its surface is wrinkled and rippled

24. for

25.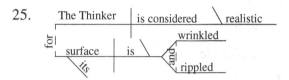

26. *The Thinker*

27. several, ones, both, many, few, others

28. [no quotation marks needed]

29. The docent explained, "The French people began to appreciate Rodin's works."

30. The Thinker

LESSON 83 The Hyphen: Compound Nouns, Numbers

Practice 83

a. already

b. all ready

c. go-getter

d. write-up

e. twenty-three, fifty-four

f. 15–21

More Practice 83

1. twenty-five

2. forty-seven

3. seventy-six

4. ninety-eight

5. twenty-first

6. thirty-second

7. forty-fifth

8. eighty-third

9. self-confidence

10. cave-ins

11. father-in-law, stand-in

12. know-it-all

Review Set 83

1. where

2. wear

3. semicircle

4. semi-

5. He

6. sat

7. most

8. nearby

9. quotation

10. dash

11. any

12. hyphen

13. fragment

14. became

15. Americans

16. different

17.   movies | were \ different

18. On Friday, my friends and I are going to see Charlie Chaplin's famous movie *City Lights*.

19. yet

20. man

21.

22. throughout the *world, with *"The Little Tramp"

23. was recognized, intransitive

24. himself

25. himself

26. all, none, any, some, most

27. The cinema teacher said, "He would always bounce back from disaster, and he never lost dignity or his sense of hope."

28. [no quotation marks needed]

29. Many readers enjoy Bret Harte's short story "The Outcasts of Poker Flat."

30. The movie buff asked, "Have you seen Charlie Chaplin's *City Lights*?"
     "No," the companion replied, "but I have seen *Modern Times*."

LESSON 84   Adverbs That Tell "How"

Practice 84

a. "peacefully" modifies "settled"

b. "rapidly" modifies "can burn"

c. "quickly" and "easily" modify "completed"

d. adjective, modifies "principal"

e. adverb, modifies "Did speak"

f. adjective, modifies "she"

g. adverb, modifies "was singing"

h. heel

i. heal

Review Set 84

1. Hemispheres

2. hemiplegia

3. hemistich

4. is

5. were

6. know

7. which

8. he

9. those

10. any

11. emphasis

12. anything

13. Both horses and mules are capable of pulling plows.

14. spent, transitive

15. were equipped, intransitive

16. assortment

17. phrase

18. automobile

19. Americans

20.

21. Electric lights, electric heat, and the Model T Ford changed American life.

22. In 1908, Henry Ford, an American businessman, manufactured a car called a Model T.

23. Look in the encyclopedia under "Ford, Henry," to find information on the Model T.

24. The Model T, they say, was well built and inexpensive.

25. Most; plural

26. "London Bridge" is a song many of us learn as children.

27. The Canterbury Tales

28. great-grandfather, do-gooder

29. Adverbs

30. how

Lesson 85   Using the Adverb *Well*

Practice 85

a. well

b. good

c. well

d. good

e. well

f. metal

g. mettle

h. medal

i. meddle

More Practice 85

1. well

2. well

3. well

4. good

5. good

6. good

7. well

8. good

9. well

10. good

Review Set 85

1. four

2. for

3. many

4. rite

5. grew

6. least

7. This

8. indefinite

9. -ly

10. good

11. well

12. rebel, (is) rebelling, rebelled, (has) rebelled

13.

14. people's

15. Despite my *work; on the *fence

16. At the *deli; on the *corner; on *rye; with *mustard

17. Last, September, Xana, Haldor, Thessaloniki, Greece

18. Snowball and Snicker

19. stalked and attacked

20.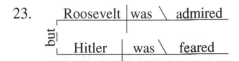

21. The noisy, crowded flea market was full of bargains.

22. bicyclists

23. frequented, transitive

24. What

25. who

26. Examples: softly, slowly, quietly, gently, lovingly, quickly, etc.

27. Examples: hard, fast, right, early, long

28. adverb

29. adjective

30. adjective

LESSON 86   The Hyphen: Compound Adjectives

Practice 86

a. G-rated

b. none

c. re-pair

d. forty-meter

e. rain-soaked

f. creak

g. creek

Review Set 86

1. metals

2. heal

3. mettle

4. already

5. thrown

6. knows

7. mice

8. warmer

9. hyphen

10. hyphen

11. Adverbs

12. "where"

13. exclamatory

14. put, transitive

15. had confessed

16. Dear Lenora,
    When you visit Mother and me in Tennessee this spring, don't forget to bring your journal.
    Love,
    James

17. principal, colder, warmer

18. Neither/nor

19. Roosevelt was admired

20. Hitler was feared

21. but

22. Roosevelt was admired, but Hitler was feared.

23.
```
     ┌ Roosevelt │ was \ admired
   but│
     └ Hitler    │ was \ feared
```

24. He, nominative

25. [answer given: How?]

26. When?

27. Where?

28. How much?

29.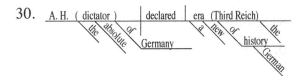

30.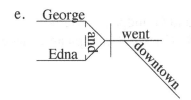

LESSON 87   Adverbs That Tell "Where"

Practice 87

a. somewhere; was hiding

b. home; had come

c. inside; might have been staying

d. around; jumped

e.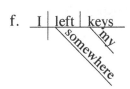

f.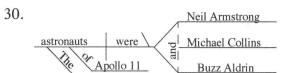

g. minor

h. minor

i. miner

Review Set 87

1. medals

2. meddle

3. all ready

4. vain

5. drew

6. suggests

7. he

8. twenty-one

9. hyphen

10. "how"

11. Well

12. Good

13. moon

14. occurs

15. have been studying

16. February

17. The

18. good

19. On July 20, 1969, three astronauts were orbiting the moon.

20. When . . . bleu cheese, thousand island, or French dressing . . . salads, tell him I . . . vinegar and oil.

21. President Kennedy's goal was achieved

22. when the 1969 moon landing was successful

23. when

24. When the 1969 moon landing was successful, President Kennedy's goal was achieved.

25. them, people

26. He

27. (a) peaceful, peacefully
    (b) harmful, harmfully

28. hard, fast, right, long, early

29. outside, ahead, around, away, there

30.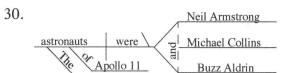

LESSON 88 — Word Division

Practice 88

a. no division

b. ab- sence

c. choco- late

d. no division

e. no division

f. twenty- seven

g. past

h. passed

More Practice 88

1. no division
2. dia- meter
3. epi- taph
4. no division
5. cir- cular *or* circu- lar
6. anti- freeze
7. no division
8. nec- essary *or* neces- sary
9. pru- dence
10. semi- circle
11. no division
12. frac- ture
13. han- gar
14. poly- gon
15. post- war
16. no division
17. mas- sive
18. no division
19. hemi- sphere
20. anti- septic

Review Set 88

1. vane
2. allegation
3. allegiance
4. razed
5. led
6. she
7. they
8. her
9. Some
10. well
11. good
12. prepositions
13. adverbs
14. run-on sentence
15. Grandma and Grandpa . . . Memorial Day parade. One . . . Grandpa and Uncle Roy . . . float.
16. grew
17. Germany, France, Austria, Europe
18. sugar
19. After the *storm, on the *horizon
20. America's, big, small, front
21. I.   Breeds of dogs
     A. Working breeds
     B. Sporting breeds
22. Juliet
23. If you're brave, take the long, dark road through the forest.
24. him
25. theirs
26. themselves
27. hyphen
28. hyphen

29.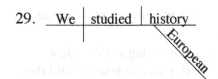

30.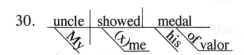

LESSON 89   Adverbs That Tell "When"

Practice 89

a. Tonight, will study

b. early, will come

c. Yearly; pays

d. tomorrow; will fill

e.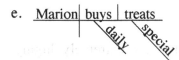

f.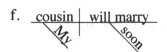

g. lose

h. loss

i. loose

Review Set 89

1. ultra-

2. in-

3. dia-

4. sub-

5. slept

6. she

7. Who

8. well watered

9. well-watered

10. well

11. phrase

12. flew, past tense

13. were

14. world

15. fortitude

16. Charles Lindbergh, Atlantic Ocean

17. After thirty-three *hours,
    in the *air,
    with his *fingers

18. American

19. The name of C. Lindbergh's plane was
    the <u>Spirit of St. Louis</u>.

20. For your information, as his little plane
    shook in the wind, Charles Lindbergh
    flew through deep, dense fog, clouds,
    and thunderstorms before he landed in
    Paris, France.

21. who

22. We

23. Nobody

24. This

25. one-way

26. true

27. Yesterday, slowly, cautiously, uphill

28. preposition

29. adverb

30.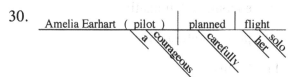

LESSON 90   Adverbs That Tell "How Much"

Practice 90

a. very; serious

b. extremely; endangered

c. quite; rapidly

d. so; necessary

e. n't; do know

f. allowed

g. aloud

h. allowed

i.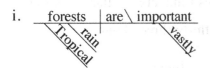
forests | are \ important
Tropical rain
vastly

j.
We | must protect | environment
our
diligently
very

More Practice 90 *See answers on page 185.*

Review Set 90

1. affect

2. feints

3. polysyllabic

4. prodigious

5. good

6. were

7. was

8. will study

9. encouraged, transitive

10. played, intransitive

11. family

12. You . . . South Dakota.

13. minutes

14. but

15. Mrs. Polly, the new librarian, asked, "Children, how many Mother Goose poems do you know?"

16. "Do you know," asked the historian, "what flag has endured the longest without change?"

17. "Let's look it up!" cried an interested visitor.
    "The Danish flag is the oldest unchanged flag in existence," said the historian.

18. <u>Dannebrog</u>

19. Who knows what country has a flag with a large white cross on a red background?

20. This . . . nation—Denmark.

21. 100–200

22. dictionary

23. A

24. lovely, lively, friendly, orderly, lonely

25. everywhere

26. yearly

27. totally, completely, extremely, highly, partly

28.
woman | appeared \ stern
The young

29.
you | Have memorized | rhyme
that

30.
crackers | taste \ stale
These
rather

LESSON 91 Comparison Adverbs

Practice 91

a. more loudly

b. most quickly

c. better

d. hardest

e. worse, worst

f. weather

g. whether

h. whether

More Practice 91

1. better

2. best

3. farther

4. less

5. least

6. slower

7. longer

8. harder

Review Set 91

1. past

2. lose

3. miners

4. creaked

5. ate

6. remember

7. Adverbs

8. Well

9. Good

10. superlative

11. positive

12. exclamatory

13. sentence fragment

14. <u>was</u> eating

15. will put, transitive

16. I.   Little Jack Horner
    A. Sat in a corner
    B. Ate a Christmas pie

17. The, Christmas, a, round, ripe, juicy

18. We can write 75¢ in decimal form as $0.75.

19. Amy

20. she

21. who

22. thirty-two

23. caramel-filled

24. often, not [or n't]

25. immediately

26. shouldn't

27. break- fast

28. sel- dom

29.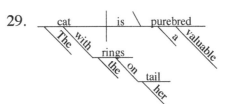

30.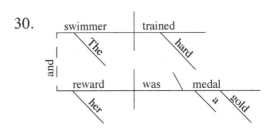

LESSON   The Semicolon
92

Practice 92

a. Homophone pairs . . . coarse, course; stationary, stationery; . . . .

b. Tomatoes . . . farms; . . . .

c. Many . . . vegetables; . . . .

d. blue

e. blue

f. blew

g. blew

More Practice 92   *See answers on page 186.*

Review Set 92

1. allowed
2. loss
3. passed
4. Minors
5. ran
6. are
7. Adverbs
8. well
9. good
10. comparative
11. superlative
12. Queen of Hearts
13. had made
14. 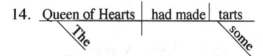 Queen of Hearts | had made | tarts — The ... some
15. (is) calling
16. (has) grown
17. Hey, Queen, Hearts
18. Her, the
19. hot, hotter, hottest
20. tarts
21. Dear King,

    The Knave of Hearts has promised not to steal tarts ever again. Therefore, you needn't punish him any more.
    Gratefully,
    The Queen of Hearts
22. B
23. we
24. "I remind people to make a note of where the bus is parked," the tour guide said, "but they always think they can remember."
25. none
26. uten- sil

27. confidently, enthusiastically
28. most
29. King of Hearts | wanted | tarts — The really those
30. Aunt Janine — traveled north / and / attended | college

LESSON 93   **Descriptive Adverbs • Adverb Usage**

Practice 93

a. dear
b. deer
c. dear
d. Example: speedily
e. Example: carefully
f. surely
g. really
h. really
i. badly
j. badly

More Practice 93

1. surely
2. really
3. certainly
4. really
5. really
6. badly
7. bad
8. badly
9. well
10. bad

Additional Practice 93   *See "Silly Story #5" on pages 187–188. Answers will vary.*

Review Set 93

1. aloud

2. loose

3. creek

4. metal

5. told

6. best

7. Whom

8. has

9. any

10. clause

11. baked

12. cake

13. me

14.

15. In, South

16. Mississippi

17. and, but, or, for, nor, yet, so

18. I wanted to see Yosemite National Park, Jeff hoped to visit Yellowstone, but we're going to Mount Rushmore.

19. The Golden Gate Bridge, I understand, is considered one of the most remarkable engineering achievements of the twentieth century.

20. visited; transitive

21. "What type of bridge is the Golden Gate?" asked the curious tourist.
     The guide responded, "It is a suspension bridge."

22. (a) how much
    (b) where
    (c) how
    (d) when

23. adjective

24. all-knowing

25. another adverb

26. adjective

27. verb

28. er, est

29. more, least

30. Orange . . . warm climate; . . . .

LESSON 94   The Colon

Practice 94

a. Please . . . 7:00 a.m.

b. Students . . . following subjects: . . . .

c. Dear Madam: . . . .

d. Martin Luthor King . . . words: . . . .

e. pair

f. pear

g. pare

Review Set 94

1. heel

2. Already

3. vein

4. icons

5. has

6. anything

7. any

8. intensifiers

9. adverb

10. adverb

11. adjective

12. surely

13. follow, (is) following, followed, (has) followed

14. had followed

15. had been enforcing

16. appeared

17. Some, Mary, Had, Little, Lamb

18. I, Mary

19. white

20. a little white lamb

21. The energetic, imaginative Franklin Delano Roosevelt was the only man to be elected President four times.

22. Franklin D. Roosevelt . . . four times—1932, ...

23. These

24. faithfully

25. not, quite, very, rather, somewhat, too

26. Eleanor Roosevelt . . . woman; she . . . .

27. courageously

28. The mail carrier . . . 8:00 a.m. daily.

29.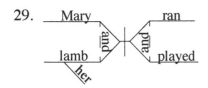

30.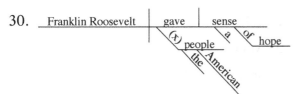

LESSON 95   The Prepositional Phrase as an Adverb • Diagramming

Practice 95

a. through hard work; develops

b. on a small farm; was born

c. with sunshine; comes

d. of your plans; were aware

e. concerning nutrition; wise

f.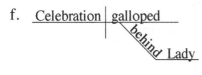

g.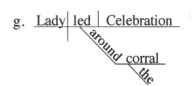

h. sight

i. cite

j. site

More Practice 95

1.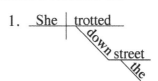

2.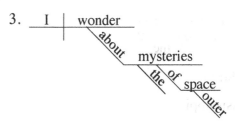

3.

4. to a *heap

5. on the *lawn, in a *dress

Review Set 95

1. anxious

2. scent

3. consequence

4. prodigious

5. has

6. most

7. adjective

8. adverb

9. really

10. badly

11. jumped, intransitive

12. watched, transitive

13. collection

14. dog's

15. dishes

16. echoes or echos

17. over the *moon

18. with the *spoon

19. from the *Columbia*

20. Neither/nor

21. "When learning to waltz," the dance instructor said, "count 1-2-3 in your head."

22. Yours

23. one

24. Eagle, Columbia

25. here, still, almost, now, quite

26. Gerardo hoped to visit Paris, France; London, England; and Dublin, Ireland.

27. Gentlemen: . . . ?

28. over the bridge; galloped

29.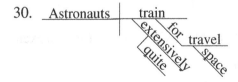

30. Astronauts | train

LESSON 96   Preposition or Adverb? • Preposition Usage

Practice 96

a. adverb

b. preposition

c. preposition

d. adverb

e. in

f. Between

g. besides

h. perennial

i. semiannual

j. annual

Review Set 96

1. cite

2. pears

3. dear

4. blew

5. exclamatory

6. active

7. was

8. any

9. ours

10. well

11. sentence fragment

12. Have you seen Georgie Porgie?

13. they cried

14. Whenever Georgie Porgie kissed the girls

15. Whenever

16. Has been kissing

17. girls

18. Georgie Porgie | Has been kissing | girls

19. kiss, (is) kissing, kissed, (has) kissed

20. audacity

21. The playground supervisor cautioned Georgie Porgie, "You must stop kissing the girls."

22. Sister Maria taught mathematics, Chinese, and music at St. Mark's Catholic School.

23. Dear Brother Phillip,
    I, Pacific Northwest, Tomorrow, Puget
    Sound, I, I, I, Mount Rainier,
    Warmly, Stefania

24. Hard-working, tireless, many

25. Could purchase, transitive

26. objective case

27. Collier

28. "Little Red Riding Hood" is a fairy
    tale . . . .

29. rather

30. adverb

LESSON 97 The Apostrophe: Possessives

Practice 97

a. triangle

b. tripod

c. mothers-in-law's

d. Megan's

e. horses'

f. friends'

g. child's

h. bus's

More Practice 97

1. unicycle's

2. principal's

3. desert's

4. suburb's

5. sibling's

6. hemisphere's

7. story's

8. metal's

9. deer's

10. rays'

11. miners'

12. fish's

13. boys'

14. sheep's

15. ladies'

16. men's

Review Set 97

1. weather

2. blue

3. deer

4. pair

5. Do

6. does

7. doesn't

8. was

9. berries

10. wives

11. hardest

12. their

13. Jack Sprat

14. could eat

15. could

16. Jack Sprat | could eat | fat
    no

17. break, (is) breaking, broke, (has) broken

18. seem

19. wife

20. Jack Sprat | gave | fat
    (x) wife / the / his

21. Jack, Sprat,
    His,
    And,
    They

22. The title, I believe, is "Jack Sprat."

23. I. Jack Sprat
    A. Jack—lean
    B. Wife—fat

24. Dust Bowl

25.

26. farms

27. nominative

28. itself

29. This

30. lived

LESSON 98   **The Apostrophe: Contractions, Omitting Digits and Letters**

Practice 98

a. weren't

b. I'm, livin', livin'

c. '74

d. 7's

e. shouldn't

f. they'd

g. one

h. unique

i. unicorn

j. prefixes

k. unify

More Practice 98   *See answers on page 189.*

Review Set 98

1. site

2. all ready

3. vain

4. heal

5. does

6. tore

7. nominative

8. they

9. who

10. clause

11. *Answers will vary.*
   Although he sings for his supper, ...

12. will have solved

13. will have been searching

14. ate; transitive

15. sang; intransitive

16. Little Tommy Tucker has no wife. [or]
   Little Tommy Tucker hasn't a wife.

17. singer

18.

19. Despite Roosevelt's *successes,
   of his new *agencies

20. Under *Roosevelt,
   for the *poor

21. simple

22.

23. of the Social Security Act

24. purpose

25. Before the Social Security Act, many Americans worried that job loss, old age, or illness might leave them in poverty.

26. No one, something, nothing

27. self-confidence

28. The average person's . . . typing; . . . .

29. I've

30.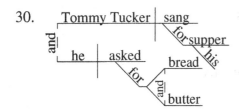

LESSON 99   The Complex Sentence • The Compound-Complex Sentence

Practice 99

a. simple

b. compound-complex

c. complex

d. compound

e. remember

f. report

g. renew

h. renew

More Practice 99

1. complex

2. compound

3. simple

4. compound-complex

Review Set 99

1. sighted

2. medals

3. vane

4. alleged

5. coordinating conjunction

6. subordinate

7. complex

8. compound-complex

9. ran

10. Those

11. I

12. really

13. and, but, or, for, nor, yet, so

14. and

15. while, as, even though, before, though

16. compound-complex

17. simple

18. Willie Winkie, Miami, Florida

19. streets

20. energetic, loud

21.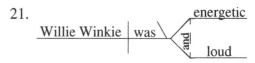

22. better

23. biggest

24. our school librarian

25. (a) mouse's
    (b) bees'
    (c) chilren's

26. My favorite dish, spaghetti, is made with tomatoes, onions, and garlic.

27. Ivanhoe, a book by Sir Walter Scott, takes place in thirteenth-century England.

28. into the pool

29.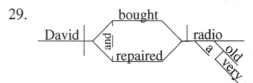

30.

LESSON 100   Active or Passive Voice

Practice 100

a. passive

b. active

c. passive

d. active

e. verify

f. verity

g. veritable

Review Set 100

1. mettle

2. Meddling

3. allegiance

4. suburbs

5. equal

6. lost

7. shook

8. fetch

9. passive

10. Passive

11. passive

12. active

13. active

14. either/or,
    neither/nor,
    both/and,
    not only/but aso

15. Either/or

16.
    Jack
    Jill
    Either or will fetch pail a of water

17. after, while, in order that, whenever, as if

18. complex

19. Jack and Jill

20.
    pair (Jack and Jill) went
    The up hill the

21. passive

22. active

23. When Mr. Parsons moved to St. Petersburg, he became interested in architecture.

24. Dear Tom and Christina,
    Unless you have other plans, please join us for dinner at 7:00. We're having tamales, your favorite.
    Warmly,
    Mom

25. possessive case

26. Who

27. You're not serious, are you?

28. (a) anti- freeze
    (b) clock- wise
    (c) cannot be divided

29. Before the United States . . . the following countries: . . . .

30.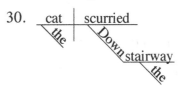
    cat scurried
    the Down stairway the

LESSON 101   **Parentheses • Brackets**

Practice 101

a. [Anne Frank]

b. ($200)

c. (a book to read or a puzzle)

d. (we hoped she would)

e. antitoxin

f. anti-

g. Antihistamines

Review Set 101

1. annual

2. semiannual

3. implied

4. eager

5. haven't

6. agrees

7. used

8. You're

9. adverbs

10. well

11. apostrophe

12. parentheses

13. can unify, transitive

14. declarative

15. (a) babies
    (b) children
    (c) boys

16. In the *1800s,
    as the first *user,
    of the *phrase

17. I believe . . . Dr. Foster . . . 9 a.m.

18. Mother Goose

19. (a) faithful
    (b) faithfully

20. not, that, far, again

21. today

22. more, carefully

23. clumsily

24. partly

25. to his middle; rose

26. adverb

27. Darryl examined . . . five-dollar bill; . . . .

28. The four words . . . as follows: . . . .

29. (a) sons'
    (b) daughters'
    (c) brothers'

30.

LESSON 102   Interjections

Practice 102

a. Okay

b. Hey

c. Bam, Pow

d. Yuck

e. Yippee | We | won | game — the

f. Oops | I | made | mistake — a

g. Sometimes

h. sometime

i. some time

j. sometime

Review Set 102

1. unicorn

2. tripod

3. anything

4. biannual

5. Good

6. contraction

7. parentheses

8. interjection

9. elephants

10. Do fear

11. mice

12. elephants | Do fear | mice — really

13. curator

14. At a *park,
    in *Washington,
    to the numerous *mice,
    in their *barns

15. no, the, the

Teacher Guide
Student Edition Answers

16. (a) and
    (b) that

17. complex

18. Some people still believe

19. (that) elephants are afraid of mice

20. herself

21. itself

22. Little Miss Muffet screamed, "There's a spider!"

23. Afterward, more, cautiously

24. terribly

25. Yesterday, away

26. preposition

27. Almonds are nuts; . . . .

28. In most . . . 10:10 . . . .

29. (a) teachers'
    (b) nurses'
    (c) presidents-elect's

30.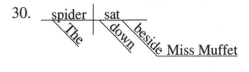

LESSON 103   Spelling Rules: Silent Letters
            k, *g*, *w*, *t*, *d*, and *c*

Practice 103

a. wrestle

b. whose

c. gnashing

d. knife

e. knot

f. knees

g. scenery

h. thistle

i. faith

j. fidelity

Review Set 103

1. verified

2. renew

3. unify

4. triangle

5. third

6. second

7. began

8. anything

9. Well

10. more

11. Besides

12. after

13. eight

14. run-on sentence

15. In the *year,
    before each leap *year,
    of the *year

16. shortest

17. Not only/but also

18. complex

19. who

20. phrase

21. beautifully

22. daily

23. too

24. like a gallant knight, rides

25. Red apples taste delicious; . . . .

26. There are . . . Saturday: . . . .

27. (a) shark's
    (b) Mr. Jones's
    (c) Benito's

28. don't

29. whistle

30.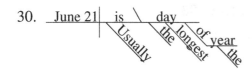
    June 21 | is \ day
    Usually | the | longest | of year | the

LESSON 104

Spelling Rules: Silent Letters
p, b, l, u, h, n, and *gh*

Practice 104

a. g<u>u</u>ess

b. althou<u>gh</u>

c. c<u>h</u>orus

d. r<u>h</u>yme

e. cou<u>l</u>d

f. ca<u>l</u>f

g. s<u>c</u>epter

h. corp<u>s</u>

i. <u>p</u>neumonia

j. de<u>b</u>t

k. tom<u>b</u>

l. yo<u>l</u>k

m. forbearance

n. patience

Review Set 104

1. forbearance

2. veritable

3. remember

4. unique

5. phrase

6. a

7. brought

8. he

9. well

10. between

11. was popularized; passive

12. of chop suey; meaning

13. Chinese

14. Pork, beef, chicken, celery, onions, noodles, and sprouts are some of the ingredients found in chop suey.

15. Mr. Wu, did you know that this special dish, chop suey, is practically unknown in China?

16. three-fourths

17. everywhere, recently

18. they found a dozen eggs

19. When they checked the nest

20. When

21. me

22. A cat . . . muscles; . . . .

23. I need . . . school: . . . .

24. (a) Bob and Chris's
    (b) hens'
    (c) gentlemen's

25. she'd

26. A dime . . . (118) . . . .

27. (a) gnat
    (b) guard
    (c) limb

28. Ugh goodbyes | are \ difficult
    so

29. Wow Hickety Pickety | was laying | eggs
    everywhere

30. chef | served | chop suey
    The (x) friends Li's American

Practice 105

a. plentiful

b. drowsiness

c. dreariest

d. happily

e. careful

f. moving

g. likely

h. timer

i. knowledgeable

j. writing

k. blameless

l. frugal

m. frugally

n. frugality

Review Set 105

1. verity

2. again

3. one

4. patience

5. Who

6. surely

7. into

8. studying

9. we cannot know for certain the date of the invention of ice cream

10. Although we can guess

11. Although

12. Italy

13. us

14. more

15. Dear Cory,
    In America, ice cream was first advertised by a man named Hall on June 8, 1786.
    Sincerely,
    Amanda

16. There is, I believe, a record of Mrs. Johnson serving ice cream at a ball in New York on December 12, 1789.

17. well-kept

18. here

19. best

20. beautifully

21. in her garden; worked
    for fun; worked

22. Los Angeles . . . California; . . . .

23. I want one thing for my birthday: . . . .

24. (a) bass's
    (b) alto's and tenor's
    (c) choir directors'

25. '01

26. The *Architeuthis* (giant squid) . . . .

27. (a) <u>w</u>ritten
    (b) <u>k</u>not
    (c) plum<u>b</u>er

28. m

29.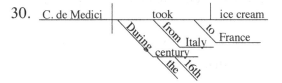

30.

Practice 106

a. snapped

b. topping

c. sadly

d. befitted

e. gladness

f. generous

g. generosity

h. generously

Review Set 106

1. fidelity

2. sometime

3. Sometimes

4. some time

5. told

6. well

7. really

8. brackets

9. me

10. have overestimated

11. species

12. The, East Africa

13. phrase

14. Remember, I spotted the elusive, reclusive short-eared owl on March 4, 2002.

15. The veterinarian asked, "Have you fed, washed, weighed, and measured your elephant?"

16. Wally replied, "No, I haven't had time to do all that."

17. precariously

18. Suddenly, down

19. Throughout the day, glued

20. preposition

21. Tigers have striped fur; they also . . . .

22. The following . . . *David Copperfield:* "The . . . ."

23. (a) spiders'
    (b) sheep's
    (c) cattle's

24. they're

25. Oops

26. (a) lam<u>b</u>
    (b) <u>k</u>nee
    (c) pa<u>t</u>ch

27. *l*

28. (a) said
    (b) paid
    (c) laid

29. dropped

30.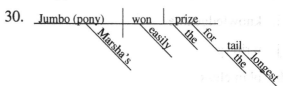

LESSON 107   Spelling Rules: *ie* or *ei*

Practice 107

a. priest

b. niece

c. deceive

d. perceive

e. freight

f. reign

g. procrastinate

h. procrastinator

i. procrastination

Review Set 107

1. procrastination

2. generous

3. frugality

4. faith

5. is

6. well

7. better

8. really

9. receipt

10. gripped

11. has been recording

12. phrase

13. Miss Myrtus, The United States Forest Service

14. I, Uncle Bill, California, May

15. Firs, poplars, and cottonwoods grow very tall.

16. Valentine

17. "Curly Locks" is the name . . . .

18. through the door; went

19. adverb

20. I am . . . Jane; . . . .

21. You . . . choices: . . . .

22. (a) men's
    (b) women's
    (c) children's

23. John's, *A*'s

24. In . . . character said, "I think she [meaning Mrs. Wu] . . . ."

25. false

26. (a) thum<u>b</u>
    (b) ta<u>l</u>k
    (c) <u>w</u>riting

27. *u*

28. truly

29. plateful

30.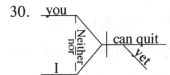

Writing Lessons Answer Key

WRITING LESSON 1
The Sentence

1. My cousin Daisy cares for many animals.
2. She feeds chickens, horses, and pigs.
3. That little pig escaped from the pen.
4. The news surprised them.
5. The assignment had confused Lulu.
6. Rembrandt painted that picture.

WRITING LESSON 2
The Paragraph, Part 1

a. Tucker is a poet!
b. The discoveries of several scientists over many years resulted in the telephones we use today.
c. Jeremy wants a strong, healthy body in order to become a firefighter someday.
d. ~~My cat's name is Whiskers.~~
e. ~~Spiders have eight legs.~~
f. ~~Herons have long, pointed bills.~~
g. That tall tree has lost its leaves.
h. We can identify trees and shrubs.
i. Everyone had a good time.
j. Many people appreciate Molly's artwork.

WRITING LESSON 3
The Paragraph, Part 2

a. 3, 4, 1, 2
b. *[Students' paragraphs will vary.]*

c. I appreciate the many advantages of train travel.
d. ~~His best friend repairs computers.~~
e. Linda has pretty brown eyes.
f. Snakes slither and slide and hide under rocks.
g. Most people like Maddy's singing.
h. The public can tour the old house.

WRITING LESSON 4
The Paragraph, Part 3

a. 3, 5, 1, 4, 2
b. *[Students' answers will vary.]*
c. Bradley designs robotic toys.
d. ~~Trina has two intelligent sisters, who are like walking encyclopedias.~~
e. Rita wore an elegant satin vest. [or] Rita wore an elegant vest made of satin.
f. I rode my bicycle to the market, to the post office, and to the library.
g. My statement confused him.
h. The goose must have startled Daisy's older sister.

WRITING LESSON 5
The Essay: Three Main Parts

a. 1, 4, 3, 2
b. *[Students' paragraphs will vary.]*
c. David is an enthusiastic musician.
d. ~~Her friend Tracy is allergic to bee stings.~~
e. Quan was slicing a shiny red apple.

f. My cousins fish at Big Bear Lake, at the Kern River, and at the local reservoir.

g. The governor commented on the voters' poor turnout.

h. Our local orchestra performed that Haydn sonata.

i. Introductory Paragraph
Body Paragraph
Body Paragraph
Body Paragraph
Concluding Paragraph

WRITING LESSON 6
The Essay: Introductory Paragraph

a. <u>Three of the most annoying house pests are the termite, the flea, and the ant.</u>

b. 1, 3, 4, 2

c. *[Students' paragraphs will vary.]*

d. <u>My friends and I plan to beautify our school.</u>

e. ~~Mrs. Dalia volunteers at the hospital.~~

f. A jellyfish has long, poisonous tentacles.

g. My cousin Nick plays the guitar and the bass.

h. Uncle James painted that portrait.

i. Introductory Paragraph
   1. Introductory sentence
   2. Thesis statement
Body Paragraph
Body Paragraph
Body Paragraph
Concluding Paragraph

WRITING LESSON 7
The Essay: Body Paragraphs

a. *[Students' topic sentences will vary.]*

b. *[Students' paragraphs will vary.]*

c. <u>My cat, dog, and guinea pig all gave birth on the same day.</u>

d. 2, 1, 4, 3

e. <u>Mammals have certain characteristics that make them different from other animals.</u>

f. ~~Katy used to have a hamster.~~

g. Clara zipped up her wool jacket.

h. My classmate Robert is learning to cook.

i. Phil and Jenny husk the corn.

j. Introductory Paragraph
   1. Introductory sentence
   2. Thesis statement
Body Paragraph
   Topic sentence
   1. Supporting sentence
   2. Supporting sentence
   3. Supporting sentence
Body Paragraph
   Topic sentence
   1. Supporting sentence
   2. Supporting sentence
   3. Supporting sentence
Body Paragraph
   Topic sentence
   1. Supporting sentence
   2. Supporting sentence
   3. Supporting sentence
Concluding Paragraph

WRITING LESSON 8
The Essay: Concluding Paragraph

a. *[Students' concluding paragraphs will vary.]*

b. <u>The friends that we choose now can greatly affect the rest of our lives.</u>

c. 2, 4, 1, 3

d. <u>Hector feels very nervous about the speech that he must give in front of the whole class in just twenty minutes.</u>

e. ~~Carl used to ride racehorses.~~

f. Alma repaired the engine of the gigantic yellow school bus.

g. The waves wash driftwood to shore.

h. Introductory Paragraph
   1. Introductory sentence
   2. Thesis statement
  Body Paragraph
   Topic sentence
    1. Supporting sentence
    2. Supporting sentence
    3. Supporting sentence
  Body Paragraph
   Topic sentence
    1. Supporting sentence
    2. Supporting sentence
    3. Supporting sentence
  Body Paragraph
   Topic sentence
    1. Supporting sentence
    2. Supporting sentence
    3. Supporting sentence
  Concluding Paragraph
   1. Restatement of thesis
   2. Reference to each topic sentence
   3. Clincher sentence

WRITING LESSON 9
The Essay: Transitions

a. <u>also</u>

b. <u>Besides that</u>

c. <u>therefore</u>

d. <u>Collecting baseball cards is fun, inexpensive, and profitable.</u>

e. 2, 1, 3, 4

f. <u>Miss Nomer considers herself an expert in many areas.</u>

g. ~~Eagles and vultures are also quite large.~~

h. Dan wrote an informal, persuasive essay.

i. Talia has an iguana named Verde.

j. Parrots harvested the walnuts.

k. Introductory Paragraph
   1. Introductory sentence
   2. Thesis statement
  Body Paragraph
   Topic sentence
    1. Supporting sentence
    2. Supporting sentence

3. Supporting sentence
  Body Paragraph
   Topic sentence
    1. Supporting sentence
    2. Supporting sentence
    3. Supporting sentence
  Body Paragraph
   Topic sentence
    1. Supporting sentence
    2. Supporting sentence
    3. Supporting sentence
  Concluding Paragraph
   1. Restatement of thesis
   2. Reference to each topic sentence
   3. Clincher sentence

WRITING LESSON 10
Brainstorming for Ideas

Practice

[Students' topic sentences will vary.]

Review

a. <u>Furthermore</u>

b. <u>on the other hand</u>

c. <u>similarly</u>

d. <u>A stylist at the local beauty salon cut my hair too short.</u>

e. ~~Meteorologists predict rain for tomorrow.~~

f. The green woodpecker has a long, sticky tongue with a barbed point.

g. Miss Nomer wants to cut and style my hair.

h. The young pianist played several sonatas.

i. Introductory Paragraph
   1. Introductory sentence
   2. Thesis statement
  Body Paragraph
   Topic sentence
    1. Supporting sentence

2. Supporting sentence
3. Supporting sentence
Body Paragraph
    Topic sentence
    1. Supporting sentence
    2. Supporting sentence
    3. Supporting sentence
Body Paragraph
    Topic sentence
    1. Supporting sentence
    2. Supporting sentence
    3. Supporting sentence
Concluding Paragraph
    1. Restatement of thesis
    2. Reference to each topic sentence
    3. Clincher sentence

WRITING LESSON 13
Supporting a Topic Sentence with Experiences, Examples, Facts, and Opinions

a. *[Students' sentences will vary.]*

b. First

c. as a result

d. Therefore

e. Art is having a bad reaction to poison ivy.

f. ~~Jessica does not like peach-flavored lip gloss.~~

g. Minh sent me a short, friendly email.

h. Maria caught two rainbow trout and three bass.

i. Emil usually feeds the catfish.

j. Introductory Paragraph
    1. Introductory sentence
    2. Thesis statement
  Body Paragraph
    Topic sentence
    1. Supporting sentence
    2. Supporting sentence
    3. Supporting sentence
  Body Paragraph

Topic sentence
    1. Supporting sentence
    2. Supporting sentence
    3. Supporting sentence
Body Paragraph
    Topic sentence
    1. Supporting sentence
    2. Supporting sentence
    3. Supporting sentence
Concluding Paragraph
    1. Restatement of thesis
    2. Reference to each topic sentence
    3. Clincher sentence

WRITING LESSON 14
Supporting a Topic Sentence with Definitions, Anecdotes, Arguments, and Analogies

a–f. *[Answers will vary.]*

g. Afterward

h. however

i. Although they are twins, Penny and Jenny are very different from each other.

j. ~~Sometimes people eat chocolate-covered ants.~~

k. Kyle polished his black leather boots.

l. Half the class misunderstood the teacher's instructions.

m. Introductory Paragraph
    1. Introductory sentence
    2. Thesis statement
  Body Paragraph
    Topic sentence
    1. Supporting sentence
    2. Supporting sentence
    3. Supporting sentence
  Body Paragraph
    Topic sentence
    1. Supporting sentence
    2. Supporting sentence
    3. Supporting sentence
  Body Paragraph
    Topic sentence
    1. Supporting sentence

2. Supporting sentence
3. Supporting sentence
Concluding Paragraph
    1. Restatement of thesis
    2. Reference to each topic sentence
    3. Clincher sentence

WRITING LESSON 30
Developing an Outline

I. Forms of Money
  A. Bills
    1. $1 bills
    2. $5 bills
    3. $20 bills
  B. Checks
    1. Personal checks
    2. Traveler's checks
  C. Coins
    1. Pennies
    2. Nickels
    3. Dimes
    4. Quarters

WRITING LESSON 38
Writing in Response to Literature

1. Mrs. March describes the Hummel Family in such detail because she wants her daughters to joyfully sacrifice their breakfast to people truly in need. This act will demonstrate the real meaning of Christmas. Here are some of the details:

- Mrs. Hummel is a poor woman.

- She has a newborn baby.

- There are six other children.

- These children are cold.

- There is no fire.

- The Hummel Family has nothing to eat.

- The oldest boy comes to Mrs. March for help.

- The whole family needs relief from hunger and cold.

2. No one speaks for a minute because it is a struggle for the girls to decide to share their holiday meal with another family less fortunate than theirs. However, once the decision is made, the girls joyfully give their favorite foods to this needy family.

3. Possibly, one reason that the Hummel boy comes to Mrs. March for help might be that she has helped them or their neighbors some time in the past. The reader learns that Mrs. March reaches out to her neighbors. Mrs. March's compassionate heart is revealed when she gives Mrs. Hummel tea and gruel and dresses the little baby.

4. Jo's exclamatory sentence reveals her impetuous and enthusiastic personality: "I am so glad you came before we began!" We also know that Jo has a good sense of humor. She calls herself and her sisters angels with mittens and hoods. Also, Jo admits that she has been labeled as a "Sancha."

5. The reader notices that Meg quickly packs up the Christmas breakfast. She sacrifices the meal with no regrets. Also, she has a generous heart: "That's loving our neighbors better than ourselves, and I like it."

6. The reader knows that Amy "heroically" gives up the cream and the "muffings," specific items that she enjoys. "Heroic" implies gallant sacrifice.

7. The reader learns that Beth is helpful and generous. She wants to carry the food, and she "eagerly" expresses her enthusiasm for this expression of Christmas giving.

8. The reader knows that the March girls enjoy giving more than receiving because of this comment: "I think there were not in all the city four merrier people than the hungry little girls who gave away their breakfasts and contented themselves with bread and milk on Christmas morning."

9. The author uses a simile, "The girls… fed them *like so many hungry birds,…*" to convey how eagerly the hungry children ate.

10. *[Answers will vary.]*

WRITING LESSON 39
Writing in Response to Informational Text

1. John Adams wrote this informational excerpt. Because he is later elected to be the second President of the United States, the reader knows that he is very popular.

2. John Adams has a high opinion of Thomas Jefferson. He compliments Thomas Jefferson in many ways. He says that Thomas Jefferson is so "prompt, frank, explicit, and decisive upon committees and in conversation" that Thomas Jefferson "seized upon my heart." This means that Adams really respects Jefferson. Also, Adams encourages Jefferson to write the draft because he is "ten times" the better writer.

3. Thomas Jefferson shows his respect for John Adams when he agrees to write the document at Adams's insistence.

4. Both Thomas Jefferson and John Adams are highly respected men. Congress voted for Thomas Jefferson to head the committee. John Adams had one less vote.

5. The reader knows that Thomas Jefferson is a willing leader because he readily accepts the leadership of the committee. He shows his humility when he first offers the leadership position to John Adams.

Give after Lesson 10.

For 1–4, write whether the sentence is declarative, interrogative, exclamatory, or imperative.

1. A punctual worker clocks in on time. ___declarative___
(1)

2. Do you think pushing to the front of the line is being considerate? ___interrogative___
(1)

3. Stay in line. ___imperative___
(1)

4. Look out! ___exclamatory___
(1)

For sentences 5–7, circle the simple subject and underline the simple predicate.

5. Did (you) understand the moral of the story?
(2)

6. (He) found the simple subject of the sentence.
(2)

7. (Oliver Twist) worked in a workhouse.
(2)

For 8–15, circle the best word to complete each sentence.

8. I trust that Moe will complete the task because he is (humorous, (reliable), funny).
(3)

9. Good students do not ((waste), waist) time.
(5)

10. *Weight* and *wait* are ((homophones), homonyms, antonyms).
(4)

11. (*Moral, Respectful,* (*Punctual*)) means "on time."
(1)

12. A ((considerate), considerable, suspicious) person is thoughtful of others.
(1)

13. A moral person is concerned with right and (left, (wrong), grades).
(2)

14. *Respectful* means "courteous" and "(punctual, smart, (polite))."
(3)

15. The prefix *homo-* means "((same), opposite, irritable)."
(4)

For 16–18, write whether the word group is a sentence fragment, run-on sentence, or complete sentence.

16. The athlete ran his fastest mile ever. ___complete sentence___
(3)

17. Tossing his yo-yo to the ground. ___sentence fragment___
(3)

18. A complete sentence has both a subject and a predicate. ___complete sentence___
(2)

Make complete sentences from fragments 19 and 20. Answers will vary.

19. Tumbled down the hill. _____ Example: Jack and Jill tumbled down the hill.
(3, 4)

20. After combing his hair. _____ Example: John ate breakfast after combing his hair.
(3, 4)

For 21 and 22, add periods and capital letters to correct the run-on sentences.

21. Jill needs to go to the grocery store. **S**he also needs to take clothes to the cleaners.
(3, 4)

22. The tourist desires to see the Forum. **H**e also wants to see the Coliseum while visiting Los
(3, 4) Angeles.

For sentences 23 and 24, circle the action verb.

23. The volcano (erupted) furiously.
(5)

24. Hot, glowing lava (flowed) down the mountain.
(5)

25. Replace the underlined verb with one that is more descriptive:
(5)

The horse <u>went</u> down the hill.

Examples: <u>galloped, trotted, slid, bolted</u>

Give after Lesson 15.

For 1 and 2, write whether the noun is singular or plural.

1. nails _____plural_____
(10)

2. hammer _____singular_____
(10)

For 3–6, write whether the noun is feminine, masculine, indefinite, or neuter.

3. manatee _____indefinite_____
(10)

4. bull _____masculine_____
(10)

5. hen _____feminine_____
(10)

6. cage _____neuter_____
(10)

7. Circle the compound noun from this list: (horseshoe), licorice, sugar
(10)

8. Circle the possessive noun from this sentence: A Siamese (cat's) eyes appear slanted.
(10)

9. From memory, write 23 common helping verbs. _____
(9)

_____ is, am, are, was, were, be, being, been, has, have, had, may, might, must, _____

_____ can, could, do, does, did, shall, will, should, would _____

_____

10. Circle the simple subject of this sentence: (Rain) continued to pour from the threatening skies.
(2)

11. Underline the simple predicate of this sentence, and circle the helping verb:
(2, 9)

            The postman (will) <u>bring</u> the package to the door.

For 12–14, write whether the word group is a complete sentence, sentence fragment, or run-on sentence.

12. The sun peeked through the clouds then the rainbow appeared. <u>run-on sentence</u>
(3)

13. With the crispness of the air in the early morning hours before dawn. <u>sentence fragment</u>
(3)

14. Flaunting its full range of colors, the rainbow paralyzed its admirers. <u>complete sentence</u>
(3)

15. Circle each abstract noun from this list: (thought) (memory), lemon
(8)

16. Circle each collective noun from this list: (jury), pillow, (committee)
(8)

17. Unscramble these words to make an interrogative sentence.
(1)

rainbow   you   seen   have   ever   a   brilliant

Have you ever seen a brilliant rainbow?

For 18–25, circle the best word to complete each sentence.

18. Sun bathers (lie, lay) in the sun.
(10)

19. A (respectful, willpower) citizen takes down the American flag at dusk.
(3)

20. The hair of a hog is (coarse, course) rather than fine.
(8)

21. Please (lie, lay) my photo album on this table when you're finished looking at it.
(10)

22. Weston wore a belt around his (waist, waste).
(5)

23. Let's not (waist, waste) water by taking long showers.
(5)

24. When Kristina found a diamond necklace in the library, she took it to the "lost and found," for
(6) she has (geography, integrity, kleptomania).

25. Caleb will learn about rocks and minerals in his (biology, psychology, geology) class.
(7)

Give after Lesson 20.

1. For a–d, circle the correct verb form.
(15)

  (a) You (am, **are**, is)   (b) They (am, **are**, is)   (c) It (do, **does**)   (d) I (**do**, does)

For 2–7, write the plural of each noun.

2. penny ____**pennies**____
(13, 14)

3. mouse ____**mice**____
(13, 14)

4. hiss ____**hisses**____
(10, 13)

5. radio ____**radios**____
(13, 14)

6. cupful ____**cupfuls**____
(13, 14)

7. book ____**books**____
(10, 13)

8. Circle each letter that should be capitalized in the following:
(6, 12)

    william **s**hakespeare wrote these lines of poetry:

        Oh, my offense is rank, it smells to heaven.

        It hath the primal eldest curse upon 't . . .

9. Circle each helping verb in this sentence:
(9)

    I **would** **have** come sooner if you **had** called me.

For 10 and 11, circle the correct verb form to complete each sentence.

10. I (**shall**, will) drive to the airport.
(11)

11. The coach (toss, **tosses**) baseballs.
(7)

12. For a–d, write whether the noun is masculine, feminine, indefinite, neuter, or abstract.
(10)

  (a) truck ____**neuter**____   (b) holiday ____**abstract**____

  (c) grandmother ____**feminine**____   (d) uncle ____**masculine**____

13. Circle each possessive noun in this list: **children's**, boys, **boy's**, teachers, **teachers'**, ladies, **lady's**
(8, 10)

For 14–16, write whether the word group is a sentence fragment, run-on sentence, or complete sentence.

14. The squid's long, soft body with a large head and two huge eyes. ____**sentence fragment**____
(3)

15. The squid has an ink sac it helps the squid make a quick, undercover escape. ___run-on sentence___
(3)

16. A squid's eyes have characteristics similar to a human's. ___complete sentence___
(3)

17. Write whether the sentence below is declarative, imperative, interrogative, or exclamatory.
(1)

The squid is a carnivorous mollusk. ___declarative___

18. Circle the subject and underline the verb phrase (simple predicate) in sentences a and b.
(2)

(a) The giant (squid) can grow up to sixty feet long.

(b) (It) might weigh more than 1000 pounds.

Circle the correct word to complete sentences 19–25.

19. She rode a three-wheeled (bicycle, (tricycle), unicycle).
(13)

20. The prefix *bio-* means "((earth), life, under)."
(11)

21. That shaggy dog keeps scratching (it's, (its)) ears.
(15)

22. ((It's), Its) never too late to say you're sorry.
(15)

23. The prefix (*uni-*, *bio-*, (*sub-*)) means "under."
(14)

24. A unicycle has ((one), two, three) wheel(s).
(13)

25. Ryan worked each math problem very carefully, for he is (punctual, bilingual, (conscientious)).
(12)

Give after Lesson 25.

1. Circle each letter that should be capitalized in a and b.
(6, 20)

    (a) (t)he book was titled (t)he (p)eople of (p)ineapple (p)lace.

    (b) (p)atrick (h)enry cried, "(g)ive me liberty, or give me death."

2. Write whether the underlined perfect tense verb phrase is past, present, or future perfect in
(19) sentences a–d.

    (a) The girls <u>will have shopped</u> for six hours. _____future_____ perfect

    (b) Alisa <u>had failed</u> to check her phone messages. _____past_____ perfect

    (c) Elise and Oscar <u>have studied</u> for today's test. _____present_____ perfect

    (d) Jordan <u>has memorized</u> the helping verbs. _____present_____ perfect

3. Circle the four prepositions from this list of words:
(17, 18)

lie	tricycle	persevere	(to)
(with)	walk	run	(about)
jump	skip	(for)	not

4. Circle the present participle of the verb *jump*:   (has) jumped   ((is) jumping)   jumped
(16)

5. Circle the four helping verbs from this list: moral, over, clown, (have), red, suit, (should), hop, (shall),
(9) (may), loyalty

For 6–11, circle the correct verb form.

6. I ((am), are, is)
(15)

7. I ((have), has)
(15)

8. They (does, (do))
(15)

9. We ((shall), will)
(11)

10. Julian (shop, (shops))
(7)

11. Julian and I ((play), plays)
(7)

For 12–14, write the plural form of each noun.

12. mouse _____mice_____
(13, 14)

13. deer _____deer_____
_(13, 14)

14. woman _____women_____
_(13, 14)

15. For a–d, write whether the noun is masculine, feminine, indefinite, neuter, or abstract.
_(8, 10)

    (a) grandparent ___indefinite___   (b) love ___abstract___

    (c) father ___masculine___   (d) daughter ___feminine___

16. For a–d, write whether the word group is a sentence fragment, run-on sentence, or complete
₍₃₎ sentence.

    (a) The manatee is a gentle creature it spends its day resting, migrating, and grazing.
    ___run-on sentence___

    (b) The manatee is an endangered species. ___complete sentence___

    (c) The West African, Amazonian, and West Indian species. ___sentence fragment___

    (d) I've never seen a manatee have you? ___run-on sentence___

17. Write whether the sentence below is declarative, imperative, exclamatory, or interrogative.
₍₁₎

               Is the dugong a relative of the manatee? ___interrogative___

18. Circle the simple subject and underline the verb in this sentence:
₍₂₎

               The (dugong) <u>live</u> in areas around Australia.

Circle the correct word to complete sentences 19–25.

19. (Who's, (Whose)) painting is this?
₍₁₉₎

20. ((It's) Its) Mary Cassatt's painting.
₍₁₅₎

21. A prodigious nose is (broken, red, (large)).
₍₂₀₎

22. I don't know (who's, (whose)) canary that is.
₍₁₉₎

23. ((Who's) Whose) helping Karlo in the kitchen?
₍₁₉₎

24. Taylor has (to, (too), two) much homework.
₍₁₈₎

25. Remy flew ((to), too, two) Hawaii last weekend.
₍₁₈₎

Give after Lesson 30.

Circle the correct word to complete sentences 1–11.

1. The famous actor Jimmy Durante had a (reliable, (prodigious)) nose.
(20)

2. April has ((fewer), less) days than May.
(21)

3. A ((linking), helping, action) verb "links" the subject of a sentence to the rest of the predicate.
(22)

4. The sentence below is (declarative, interrogative, imperative, (exclamatory)):
(1)

That cat scratched me!

5. The following is a (sentence fragment, run-on sentence, (complete sentence)):
(3)

The cat's scratch bled.

6. This proper noun is (abstract, (concrete)): Amazon River
(8)

7. A monologue is performed by ((one), two, many) actor(s).
(25)

8. Morgan read the ((whole), hole) book in one day.
(24)

9. A mouse chewed a (whole, (hole)) in Helen's backpack.
(24)

10. The team felt they would win; their (moral, (morale)) was high.
(23)

11. Sara is kind and caring; she has (perseverance, (compassion), disdain) for the less fortunate.
(22)

12. Write the plural form of a–d:
(13, 14)

(a) penny __pennies__ (b) trout __trout__ (c) man __men__ (d) child __children__

Circle each letter that should be capitalized in 13–15.

13. (j)ulius (c)aesar commented, "(b)ut, for my own part, it was (g)reek to me."
(6, 20)

14. (w)illiam (s)hakespeare wrote *(j)ulius (c)aesar*.
(6, 20)

15. (i) saw *(j)ulius (c)aesar* performed at the (c)harleston (s)quare (t)heatre.
(6, 20)

16. Circle each preposition that you find in this sentence:
(17, 18)

The man (in) the clown costume came (with) me (to) the circus.

17. Circle the four helping verbs in this list: upon, wheel, (be) hammer, cart, (shall) (have) bag, sock,
(9) (must)

18. For a–d, circle the correct irregular verb form.
(15)

    (a) She (am, (is), are)   (b) They ((do), does)   (c) You (has, (have))   (d) He (do, (does))

19. Circle the present perfect verb phrase in this sentence: Erin (has completed) the marathon.
(19)

20. Circle the future perfect verb phrase in this sentence: Soon, Kim (will have finished) her sixth
(19) race.

21. Circle the future progressive verb phrase in this sentence: Ruth and Mitzi (will be celebrating)
(21) their fifteenth birthdays on Saturday.

22. Circle the future perfect progressive verb phrase in this sentence: This September, we (shall have
(21) been living) in Monrovia for 14 years.

Diagram the simple subject, simple predicate, and direct object of sentences 23 and 24.

23. The boy patted the dog.
(23, 25)

boy	patted	dog

24. The dog licked the boy.
(23, 25)

dog	licked	boy

25. For a and b, circle to indicate whether each word group is a phrase or a clause.
(24)

    (a) swallowed the cold milk   (phrase) clause

    (b) after the fish swam away   phrase (clause)

Give after Lesson 35.

Circle the correct word(s) to complete sentences 1–12.

1. Have you ever visited the ((Capitol), Capital) Building in Washington, D.C.?
(30)

2. The athlete's (faint, (feint)) of injury did not fool all the spectators.
(28)

3. The (progressive, (perfect)) verb tense shows action that has been completed.
(19, 21)

4. ((Articles), Pronouns) are the most commonly used adjectives, and they are also the shortest—*a,*
(28) *an, the.*

5. *His, her, their, your, its, our,* and *my* are examples of ((possessive), descriptive) adjectives.
(27, 28)

6. The sentence below is (declarative, imperative, interrogative, (exclamatory)):
(1)

There's a shark in these waters!

7. The word group below is a ((sentence fragment), run-on sentence, complete sentence):
(3)

Born with a knack for invention.

8. An incredible story is (very, (not), almost) believable.
(29)

9. My (monopoly, capital, (conscience)) makes me aware of right and wrong.
(26)

10. A thunderstorm might ((affect), effect) our outdoor activities.
(27)

11. Will the storm have an (affect, (effect)) on your activities?
(27)

12. The hungry bear opened (it's, (its)) mouth and growled.
(15)

13. Circle the abstract noun from this list: punchball, blacktop, chalkboard, (knowledge), hallway
(8)

14. Circle each possessive noun in this list: wives, (wife's) (sons'), sons, (aunt's), aunts, collies, (collie's)
(10)

15. Write the plural form of the singular noun *knife*. ___knives___
(13, 14)

For 16 and 17, circle each letter that should be capitalized.

16. (h)amlet cries, "(f)railty, thy name is woman."
(6, 20)

17. (d)ear (m)r (c)arruthers,
(6, 29)

    (w)e leave tomorrow for (n)ew (e)ngland. (i) can't wait to taste the chowder.

    (s)incerely, (m)iss (r)enner

18. Circle each preposition in this sentence: Haley, the energetic toddler (with) red hair, slid (down) the
(17, 18) slide and sat (on) the swings (in) the shade.

19. Circle the four helping verbs from this list: what, whom, (been) (did), globe, where, (should), (shall)
(9)

20. Circle the linking verb in this sentence: Another name for bananas (is) "hands with little fingers."
(22)

21. For a–d, circle the correct irregular verb form.
(15)

    (a) I (am), is, are)   (b) He (do, (does))   (c) They (has, (have))   (d) She ((has), have)

22. Circle the present progressive verb phrase in this sentence: This delicious banana (is providing)
(21) me with vitamin C and potassium.

23. For sentences a and b, write whether the verb is an action or linking verb.
(5, 22)

    (a) The captain <u>felt</u> seasick. _____linking_____   (b) She <u>felt</u> the boat rock. _____action_____

24. Circle each adjective in this sentence: (The) (brown) (velvety) rabbit sported (long), (slender) ears and (a)
(27, 28) (moist) (black) nose.

25. Fill in the diagram to the right using each word
(25, 28) of this sentence: Enthusiastic skiers appreciate
steep, beautiful mountains.

skiers	appreciate	mountains

Enthusiastic   steep beautiful

Give after Lesson 40.

Circle the correct word to complete sentences 1–11.

1. The prefix that means "through," "across," "between," or "apart" is (*mono-, homo-, dia-, bi-*).
(35)

2. The waiter will (pore, pour, poor) milk into the glasses.
(34)

3. This sentence is (declarative, imperative, interrogative, exclamatory): Drink that glass of milk
(1) now.

4. The word group below is a (sentence fragment, run-on sentence, complete sentence).
(3)

       When wood burns, energy changes to heat and light no energy is lost.

5. This word group is a (phrase, clause): because they have no legs
(24)

6. The noun or pronoun that follows a preposition is called the (subject, object, modifier) of the
(33) preposition.

7. The diameter is the distance (around, across, outside) a circle.
(35)

8. The prefix (*dia-, bio-, post-*) means "after."
(32)

9. A proper noun begins with a (capitol, capital) letter.
(30)

10. While rowing upstream, Daniel lost an (oar, ore, or).
(33)

11. *Postmortem* means "(after, before, through) death."
(32)

12. Circle the concrete noun from this list: Portuguese, language, Thanksgiving, wood, legalism
(8)

13. Circle the feminine noun from this list: grandmother, brother, physician, pen, shoe
(10)

14. Write the plural of the noun *sky*. _____skies_____
(13)

15. Circle each letter that should be capitalized in this humorous rhyme about chemical formulas:
(6, 12)

                johnny had a stomachache.
                he hasn't anymore.
                for what he thought was H_2O
                was H_2SO_4.

16. Circle the four prepositions in this sentence:
(17, 18)

       One of the fundamental laws in physics and chemistry is called the law of the conservation of
       energy.

Underline the prepositional phrase and circle the object of the preposition in sentences 17 and 18.

17. The instructor laid the test <u>on the (desk)</u>
(17, 33)

18. The snake <u>in the fourth (display)</u> is poisonous.
(17, 33)

19. Circle the word from this list that is *not* a helping verb: is, am, are, was, were, (why,) be, being,
(9)   been, has, had, have, do, does, did, shall, will, should, would, can, could, may, might, must

20. Circle the linking verb in this sentence: Most snakes (are) harmless.
(22)

21. For a–d, circle the correct irregular verb form.
(15)

   (a) we (was, (were))   (b) it (do, (does))   (c) you (has, (have))   (d) he (do, (does))

For sentences 22 and 23, underline the verb and circle the direct object if there is one. Then circle "transitive" or "intransitive." (Hint: A transitive verb has a direct object.)

22. Snakes <u>can slither</u> along the ground at up to six miles per hour. (transitive (intransitive))
(25, 32)

23. Reptiles <u>use</u> the (sun) to keep warm. ((transitive), intransitive)
(25, 32)

24. Circle the indirect object in this sentence: Mrs. Smith gave the (children) some cookies.
(35)

25. Fill in the diagram to the right using each word
(25, 35)   of this sentence: Debby's hot salsa gave her
   brother a pain in his stomach.

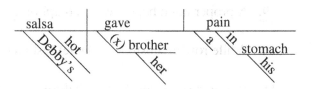

Give after Lesson 45.

Circle the correct word to complete sentences 1–12.

1. The students chose their future occupations with (prudence, perseverance, compassion).
(36)

2. Can you (so, sow, sew) my ripped seam?
(37)

3. This sentence is (declarative, imperative, interrogative, exclamatory): Have you ever seen a
(1) gopher snake?

4. This word group is a (sentence fragment, run-on sentence, complete sentence): Snakes sense
(3) vibrations they sense them with the lower jaw.

5. (Commas, Periods, Quotation marks) help the reader to know where a sentence begins and ends.
(36)

6. (Coordinating conjunctions, Verbs, Nouns) join parts of a sentence that are equal.
(37)

7. (Nouns, Adjectives, Correlative conjunctions) always come in pairs.
(39)

8. Peter chooses his friends carefully, or with (injustice, perseverance, discretion).
(36)

9. Maria and Alexandra met (there, they're, their) friend Heather at the library.
(38)

10. Please (accept, except) my apology.
(40)

11. Martin is tired, but he keeps working, for he has (independence, injustice, perseverance).
(16)

12. Nathan and Chase are talking to one another. They are having a (dialogue, diagonal, monopoly).
(35)

13. Write the plural of *piano*. _____pianos_____
(14)

14. Write the correct verb form: Jarad _____empties_____ (present tense of *empty*) the trash.
(7)

15. Circle each letter that should be capitalized in this sentence: (t)he teacher required each student to
(20) read (t)he (a)dventures of (h)uckleberry (f)inn.

16. Circle the two prepositions from this sentence: (Like) other reptiles, snakes have a backbone (of)
(17) small bones called vertebrae.

17. Circle the word from this list that is *not* a helping verb: is, am, are, was, were, be, being, been,
(9) (while), has, have, had, may, might, must, can, could, do, does, did, shall, will, should, would

18. Circle each coordinating conjunction from this list: (and), (but), (yet), seem, (or), after, not, (for), (so)
(37)

19. Circle the correlative conjunctions in this sentence: (Not only) Maria (but also) Angela attended the
(39) concert in the park.

20. Underline the prepositional phrase and circle the object of the preposition in this sentence:

(17, 33)

What is the national symbol <u>of the (United States)</u>?

21. Circle the entire verb phrase in this sentence: The football coach (has chalked) the field.

(9, 19)

22. Circle each linking verb in this list: (look), scratch, (feel), (taste) (smell), write, (sound), (seem) (appear),

(22)

cook, (grow) (become) (remain), run, (stay)

23. Add periods where they are needed in this sentence: The Rev. R. U. Glad delivered a humorous

(36)

monologue at the park on St. James St. at 9 a.m. on Sunday.

Complete the diagrams of sentences 24 and 25.

24. The flower girl gave the wedding guests rose

(25, 35) petals from her basket.

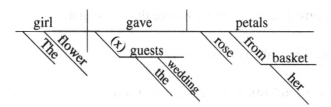

25. Tigers and leopards not only fascinate but also

(38, 39) frighten explorers.

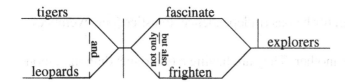

Give after Lesson 50.

Circle the correct word(s) to complete sentences 1–10.

1. The prefix *ultra-* means "(not, (extreme), after)."
(44)

2. The prefix *mal-* means "(one, life, (bad))."
(41)

3. This word group is a ((sentence fragment), run-on sentence, complete sentence): A belt around his
(3) waist.

4. She (have, (has)) two cats.
(15)

5. Positive, comparative, and superlative adjectives are known as ((comparison), descriptive)
(27, 45) adjectives.

6. The school (principle, (principal)) called a meeting of all the teachers.
(43)

7. Evelyn will (sit, (set)) her grammar book on your desk.
(42)

8. Stephen would like to ((sit) set) beside Johnny because (there, (they're), their) friends.
(42)

9. Kelly appreciates Veronica's (advise, (advice)).
(45)

10. Timothy will (so, sew, (sow)) the carrot seeds and then cover them with soil.
(37)

11. Circle the collective noun from this list: philosophy, classroom, (United Nations), thumb, Mrs.
(8) Gonzáles

Circle each letter that should be capitalized in 12 and13.

12. (t)he long novel (g)one with the (w)ind tells about life in the (s)outh during the (c)ivil (w)ar in (a)merica.
(26, 29)

13. (d)ear (a)unt (f)rances,
(26, 29)
      (i) have learned four different ways to cook okra during my visit to the (s)outh.

            (l)ove,
            (j)aime

14. The plural of the noun *prefix* is _____prefixes_____.
(13)

15. Underline the prepositional phrase and circle the object of the preposition in this sentence:
(17, 33)

            Mother's Day is a special day <u>of the</u> (year).

16. Circle the verb phrase in this sentence: Our class (will be going) to the museum on Thursday.
(9, 21)

17. For sentences a and b, write whether the underlined verb is action or linking.
(5, 22)

   (a) The music <u>sounded</u> harmonious. _____linking_____

   (b) The children <u>sounded</u> the bell when the Mother's Day breakfast was ready. _____action_____

18. Circle the two possessive adjectives in this sentence: After Anna (Jarvis's) mother passed away in
(28) 1907, Anna convinced her (mother's) church to set aside the second Sunday of May to honor all mothers.

19. Circle the correlative conjunctions in this sentence: (Not only) the church of Anna Jarvis's
(39) mother, (but also) churches across the United States began to celebrate Mother's Day.

20. Circle the predicate nominative in this sentence: Flowers are the most common (gift) on Mother's
(41) Day.

For 21–23, write whether the italicized word is nominative case, objective case, or possessive case.

21. Denmark, Finland, and Turkey, are other *countries* that celebrate Mother's Day.
(42, 43) _____nominative case_____

22. Actually, the tradition of honoring mothers dates back to ancient *Greece*. _____objective case_____
(12, 43)

23. In 1914, *President Woodrow Wilson* declared Mother's Day an official holiday.
(42, 43) _____nominative case_____

Complete the diagrams of sentences 24 and 25.

24. Fido tasted the frosting on the cake.
(25)

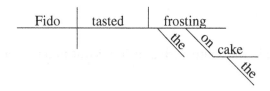

25. Mother's Day became important and meaningful.
(44, 38)

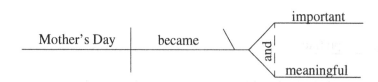

Give after Lesson 55.

Circle the correct word to complete sentences 1–13.

1. The electric company will (advice, (advise)) consumers of an upcoming blackout.
(45)

2. ((Malnutrition), Maltreatment, Maladjustment) is the result of a poor diet.
(41)

3. This word group is a (sentence fragment, run-on sentence, (complete sentence)): Have you ever
(3) fished for salmon?

4. The gender of the noun *assistant* is (masculine, feminine, (indefinite), neuter).
(10)

5. The past participle of the verb *dance* is ((danced), dancing).
(16)

6. Our electrical shortage is the (baddest, (worst)) one in several decades.
(45, 46)

7. Washington Avenue is (wide, (wider), widest) than Lincoln Boulevard.
(45)

8. A fishing expert (do, (does), done) catch many salmon.
(15)

9. Jazmyne, ((may), can) I eat lunch with you today?
(48)

10. Jack found the missing puzzle ((piece), peace) on the floor.
(49)

11. An ultraconservative person is ((very), not, slightly) conservative.
(44)

12. Tomorrow morning, Jenna will (rays, (raise), raze) the American flag again.
(46)

13. Did Jenna ((break), brake) Norman's mechanical pencil?
(47)

Circle each letter that should be capitalized in 14 and 15.

14. (h)ave you read (j)ack (l)ondon's (t)he (c)all of the (w)ild?
(6, 20)

15. (t)he largest salmon is the (p)acific salmon.
(30, 31)

16. The plural of *salmon* is _____salmon_____.
(14)

17. Circle the four words from this list that are *not* prepositions: alongside, concerning, (species),
(17) regarding, underneath, (parents), amid, below, (spawned), excepting, from, (conditions), opposite,
like, since, to

18. Underline each prepositional phrase and circle the object of each preposition in this sentence: A
(17, 33) salmon can be classified by (species), by the (river) of its (birth), and by the (season) its parents
spawned.

19. Circle the verb phrase in this sentence: Seven species of salmon ~~were experiencing~~ frightening
(21) decreases in population.

20. For sentences a and b, circle to show whether the underlined verb is transitive or intransitive.
(32)

    (a) The man <u>swam</u> the English Channel. ((transitive), intransitive)

    (b) The man <u>swam</u> steadily. (transitive, (intransitive))

21. Circle the sentence below that is written correctly.
(30)

       I like that kind of a pie.   (I like that kind of pie.)

22. Add periods and commas as needed in this sentence: The baseball fans ate popcorn, salted
(36, 47) peanuts, hotdogs, and frozen malts.

23. Write whether the italicized word in this sentence is nominative, objective, or possessive
(42, 43) case: The shortstop caught a line *drive* during the seventh inning of the baseball game.
      <u>   objective   </u> case

24. Circle the appositive in this sentence: Babe Ruth, (a famous baseball player) was inducted into
(48) the Hall of Fame many years ago.

25. Diagram this sentence in the space to the
(22, 44) right: That Boston fern looks thirsty.

    fern | looks \ thirsty

Grammar and Writing 6   **124**   **Teacher Guide**
Test Answers

Give after Lesson 60.

Circle the correct word(s) to complete sentences 1–9.

1. The pilot coasted his airplane into the (hanger, (hangar)).
(52)

2. The icemaker in our refrigerator breaks down ((continually), continuously).
(54)

3. This fish is the (baddest, (worst)) I've ever eaten!
(46)

4. I ((shall), will) study the Boer War in the near future.
(11)

5. ((Can), May) Norman tighten the hand (break, (brake)) on his bicycle?
(48, 47)

6. The value of a vehicle might (substitute, (depreciate), maltreat) as time goes on.
(53)

7. Austin and John (right, (write), wright, rite) humorous essays.
(50)

8. Allison hung Hailey's coat on a ((hanger), hangar).
(52)

9. Samuel, Dylan, and Kenneth have signed a ((peace), piece) treaty.
(49)

10. Circle the four words in this list that are *not* prepositions: inside, into, like, near, of, off, on, onto,
(17) ((flutter), (glide), opposite, out, (marine), outside, over, past, (aquarium), regarding, round

11. For sentences a and b, circle to show whether the underlined verb is transitive or intransitive.
(32)

   (a) The candle <u>glowed</u> faintly in the hallway. (transitive, (intransitive))

   (b) The roaring fire <u>consumed</u> the logs. ((transitive), intransitive)

12. Write the (a) past tense and (b) past participle of the irregular verb *drink*.
(16, 54)

   (a) _____drank_____   (b) ___(has) drunk___

13. Add commas and periods as needed in this sentence:
(49)

   Dr. Georgia L. Banks Ph.D., the chairperson of Exotic Felines, explained that there is
   actually no such cat as a panther.

14. Circle the coordinating conjunction in this sentence: Lions, tigers, leopards, (and) jaguars belong
(37) to the genus *Panthera*.

15. Write whether the italicized nouns in this sentence are nominative, objective, or possessive case:
(42, 43)

   Leopards and *jaguars* have tan coats with black spots. _____nominative_____ case

16. Circle the appositive in this sentence: Our school mascot, ⟨the black panther,⟩ is just a leopard in disguise.
(48)

17. Underline the pronoun and circle its antecedent in this sentence: Just because Max can't see the
(51) black ⟨spots⟩ on a black leopard doesn't mean <u>they</u> aren't there.

18. Circle each pronoun from this list that is third person plural: he, him, she, her, ⟨they⟩, ⟨them⟩, ⟨their⟩,
(51) his, hers

19. Circle each nominative case pronoun in this list: me, him, ⟨I⟩, ⟨she⟩, them, ⟨they⟩, ⟨he⟩, her, ⟨we⟩, us
(55)

Circle the nominative case pronoun in sentences 20 and 21.

20. The woman on the phone is (her, ⟨she⟩).
(55)

21. ⟨He⟩, Him) and Sal play soccer.
(55)

22. Circle the sentence that is more polite (a or b).
(55)

   (a) The nominees were I and he.   (b) ⟨The nominees were he and I.⟩

23. Circle each letter that should be capitalized in this sentence:
(6, 29)

   ⟨l⟩eopards can be found in ⟨a⟩frica, the ⟨m⟩iddle ⟨e⟩ast, and ⟨a⟩sia.

Diagram sentences 24 and 25 in the space to the right.

24. The zoo exhibits both leopards and jaguars.
(25, 38)

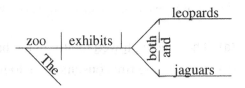

25. Leopards and jaguars are carnivorous animals.
(38, 41)

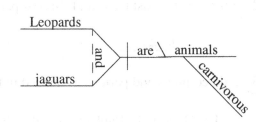

Give after Lesson 65.

Circle the correct words to complete sentences 1–14.

1. The committee believes that (your, **you're**) the best person for the job.
(56)

2. Josephine has two sisters and one brother, or three (**siblings**, hangars, pieces).
(59)

3. The following word group is a (phrase, **clause**): when one thinks of nationalism
(24)

4. Of the three countries, Italy was the (more, **most**) successful in her struggle for independence.
(46)

5. A predicate (**nominative**, subject, verb) follows a linking verb and renames the subject.
(41)

6. (**Its**, It's) leg appears to be fractured.
(15)

7. Esther and (her, **she**) walked to the shore.
(55)

8. Please go with José and (I, **me**) to deliver this meal.
(57)

9. The attendant gave Sergio and (**him**, he) the best seats in the stadium.
(57)

10. What time will the sun (raise, **rise**) tomorrow?
(58)

11. Ashley didn't have a pencil, so Patrick offered to (**lend**, borrow) her one.
(57)

12. Devin turned (**right**, write, wright, rite), not left, at the corner.
(50)

13. Please (leave, **let**) me go swimming!
(60)

14. Lauren will hang up (**your**, you're) coat for you.
(56)

15. Circle each letter that should be capitalized in this sentence: **T**he gardenia bush smells most
(30, 31) fragrant in the spring.

16. Circle the entire verb phrase in this sentence: Italy **had been united** as a nation in 1861.
(9, 19)

17. Add periods as needed in this sentence: Please deliver this check for $12**.**99 (twelve dollars and
(36, 40) ninety-nine cents) to our Lindsey St**.** office**.**

Add commas as needed to sentences 18 and 19.

18. No**,** I cannot remember the last time we were in Seattle**,** Washington.
(47, 56)

19. It rains all the time**,** I seem to recall.
(56)

20. Unscramble these words to make a sentence with a personal pronoun as a predicate nominative:
(55)

mud   in   she   the   sow   was   the

The sow in the mud was she.

21. Circle each objective case personal pronoun from this list:
(57)

(me)   (him)   I   she   (them)   they   he   (her)   we   (us)

22. Write whether the italicized pronoun in this sentence is nominative, objective, or possessive case:
(58)

Yours is around the corner.   __possessive__ case

Diagram sentences 23–25 in the space to the right.

23. Appaloosas are horses with distinct
(34, 41) markings.

Appaloosas | are \ horses
with / markings
distinct

24. Not only spots but also solid colors can
(38, 39) cover the Appaloosa.

spots
Not only / but also
colors | can cover | Appaloosa.
solid / the

25. The best riders are Jane and she.
(41, 59)

riders | are \ Jane
and
she
The / best

Give after Lesson 70.

Circle the correct words to complete sentences 1–14.

1. A golfer yells "(for, fore, four)" to warn that a golf ball is coming.
(64)

2. The restaurant offered chocolate mousse and apple cobbler for (desert, dessert).
(63)

3. A (correlative, subordinating, coordinating) conjunction introduces a dependent clause.
(61)

4. Did you score (gooder, better, best) than your opponent in the speech contest?
(46)

5. Tedmond (knowed, knew, known) every answer on the test.
(54)

6. The woman with the umbrella is (her, she).
(55)

7. The person hiding in the garden was (me, I).
(55)

8. RuthAnn's chili was superb, while (ours, our's) was just so-so.
(58)

9. They spun the wool (theirselves, themselves).
(62)

10. The prefix (*frac-, geo-, poly-*) means "many."
(61)

11. Please (teach, learn) me how to speak Russian.
(62)

12. Aaron photographs reptiles in the (desert, dessert).
(63)

13. A polygon has (long, curved, many) sides.
(61)

14. Everyone (accept, except) Adrian had the wrong answer.
(40)

15. Circle the subordinating conjunction in this sentence:
(61)

 I will persevere in my Spanish class until I have mastered the language.

16. Circle the verb in this sentence, and circle to show whether it is an action or linking verb:
(5, 22)

 In the 1860s, the king of Prussia appointed a new prime minister. (action, linking)

17. In the blanks below, write the four principal parts of the verb *snip*.
(16)

 (a) present tense: __snips__   (b) present participle: __(is) snipping__

 (c) past tense: __snipped__   (d) past participle: __(has) snipped__

18. Circle each adjective in this sentence: Prussia was a large, powerful state in Germany.
(27, 28)

19. Write whether the italicized noun in this sentence is in the nominative, objective, or possessive
(42, 43) case:

Otto von Bismarck, a nationalist, was the new *prime minister*. ___nominative___ case

20. Add commas as needed in this sentence:
(65)

"Unfortunately**,**" explained Mrs. Schmidt**,** "Bismarck was a ruthless leader."

21. Circle the appositive in this sentence: The Prussian king, (Wilhelm I) was declared Kaiser of the
(48) united German states.

22. Circle the antecedent for the italicized pronoun in this sentence:
(51)

(Bismarck) was forced from office because *he* and Wilhelm's successor did not get along.

23. Circle the sentence that is more polite (a or b).
(57)

(a) The lemon meringue pie was for him and me.

(b) The lemon meringue pie was for me and him.

Diagram sentences 24 and 25 in the space to the right.

24. Yours is the best entry at the fair.
(34, 41)

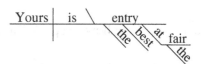

25. Most people supported the new railroad, but
(64, 65) some people disliked the noise, dirt, and
danger.

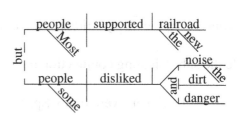

Circle the correct word to complete sentences 1–12.

1. The (arrogance, prudence, humility) of the university student offended many people.
(70)

2. José could not decide whether to attend summer school or to work a summer job. He had a
(66) (desertion, dilemma, peace).

3. A (verb, adjective, pronoun) takes the place of a noun.
(51)

4. The grateful recipient of a scholarship thanked (her, she) and them many times.
(57)

5. The sixth grader (which, who) wore size twelve shoes ran the fastest mile.
(66)

6. It was (me, I).
(55)

7. They (was, were) organized.
(15)

8. Did you (here, hear) Giancarlo's good news?
(68)

9. (Can, May) I borrow your pen?
(48)

10. The prefix (*frac-*, *hemi-*, *anti-*) means "against."
(65)

11. A polychromatic rug has (artificial, shiny, many) colors.
(61)

12. To prevent infection, Ayanna sprayed (hemistich, antiseptic, postscript) on Helen's wound.
(65)

13. Circle the entire verb phrase in this sentence:
(9, 21)

We might have been discussing the effects of a violent tornado.

14. Circle the indirect object in this sentence: The chef broiled me a swordfish steak.
(35)

15. Circle each letter that should be capitalized in this sentence:
(29, 31)

in the autumn, we see brilliant yellows, oranges, and reds on foliage in the east.

16. Circle the possessive adjective in this sentence: A strong tornado may leave its mark on the
(28, 60) landscape.

17. Circle the overused adjective in this sentence: It's neat that a tornado can drive a straw into a
(50) plank of wood.

18. Underline the dependent clause and circle the subordinating conjunction in this sentence:
(61)

Unless it snows, I'll hike Mount Whitney tomorrow.

19. Add commas as needed to this sentence: On Friday, February 6, 2003, Grandma and Grandpa's
(47, 49) fiftieth wedding anniversary, we sang their favorite song, *When Irish Eyes Are Smiling*.

20. Unscramble these words to make a sentence with a personal pronoun as an object of a
(33, 53) preposition:

him   ate   surgeon   the   with   lunch

_____The surgeon ate lunch with him._____

Circle each reflexive or intensive pronoun in sentences 21 and 22.

21. We roofed the house (ourselves)
(62)

22. A cat cleans (itself) by licking its fur.
(62)

23. Add quotation marks to this sentence: "I may never see a blue whale," the marine biologist said.
(69, 70)

Diagram sentences 24 and 25 in the space to the right.

24. Have you memorized a portion of that poem?
(25, 34)

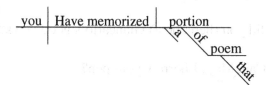

25. Do Hoover and he like pickle sandwiches with mustard?
(23, 38)

Give after Lesson 80.

Circle the correct words to complete sentences 1–16.

1. The (sympathy, (reconciliation), punctuality) of the old enemies was long overdue.
(75)

2. The tiny terrier (beared, (bared), devised) his teeth at the enormous Rottweiler.
(74)

3. The Archbishop of York has (flee, (fled)) to Canterbury.
(74)

4. Our laundry has (lied, lay, (laid)) in that same spot all morning.
(75)

5. Case indicates how ((pronouns), italics, quotation marks) are used in a sentence.
(58)

6. That hilarious e-mail I received was from William and (she, (her)).
(57)

7. They baked, frosted, and decorated the wedding cake (theirselves, (themselves)).
(62)

8. Mr. Yu, (who, (whom)) you know, will visit tomorrow.
(66, 68)

9. Amelia (teared, (tore), torn) up the silly note she wrote yesterday.
(54)

10. ((Those), Them) oatmeal cookies are the best I have ever tasted.
(71)

11. Few ((enjoy), enjoys) push-ups, sit-ups, and other physical exercises.
(72)

12. Using hotel (stationary, (stationery)), Kent wrote Jason a letter all about his vacation in Jackson
(73) Hole, Wyoming.

13. Natalie rescued Nicole from a large grizzly (bare, (bear)) in the forest.
(74)

14. Caleb, Mark, and Isaac had goosebumps, for they failed to (ware, (wear), where) warm clothing.
(72)

15. Quadrupeds are animals having (for, fore, (four)) feet.
(64)

16. Miss Curtis's driver's license had expired; therefore, it was (fractious, (invalid), semiprecious).
(55)

17. In the blanks below, write the four principal parts of the verb *shove*.
(16)

    (a) present tense: <u>_shove(s)_____</u>   (b) present participle: <u>_(is) shoving_____</u>

    (c) past tense: <u>_shoved_____</u>   (d) past participle: <u>_(has) shoved_____</u>

18. Circle each letter that should be capitalized:
(6, 26)

(m)y parents went to (n)iagara (f)alls on their honeymoon. (p)art of (n)iagara (f)alls is in (n)ew (y)ork and part of it is in (c)anada. (m)om and (d)ad told me that on (j)une 30, 1859, a (f)renchman named (j)ean (f)rancois (g)ravelet crossed the (n)iagara (r)iver (g)orge on a tightrope.

19. Underline each prepositional phrase in this sentence, and circle the object of each preposition:
(17, 33)

Whalebone is not bone, and it has none <u>of the (characteristics)</u> <u>of (bone)</u>.

20. Circle the verb in this sentence, and circle to show whether it is transitive or intransitive:
(32)

Whalebone, or baleen, (grows) on the roof of the mouth in certain whales. (transitive, (intransitive))

21. Add commas where necessary in this sentence:
(56, 63)

According to some authorities **,** the thin **,** parallel plates of baleen can reach lengths of fifteen feet.

22. Circle each word that should be italicized in this sentence:
(73)

The French say (beau) for handsome, but the Spanish say (guapo).

23. Underline the dependent clause in this sentence, and circle the subordinating conjunction:
(61)

I have more free time (than) she has.

Diagram sentences 24 and 25 in the space to the right.

24. The Archbishop of York is the Primate of
(23, 41) England.

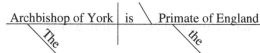

25. Certain species of whales grow whalebone.
(25, 34)

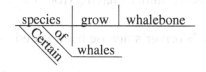

Circle the correct words to complete sentences 1–12.

1. The large number of holes in the yard (devised, (implied), razed) the presence of gophers.
(79)

2. The ((anxious), prodigious, conscientious) hikers watched dark storm clouds gather.
(78)

3. James Earle Fraser, an American sculptor, (make, (made)) the buffalo nickel with no particular
(75) Indian chief in mind.

4. ((Whoever), Whomever) made this casserole is a good cook.
(66, 68)

5. The forest ranger gave (we, (us)) Boy Scouts a guided tour of the woods.
(57, 58)

6. (Who, (Whom)) did the lifeguard rescue?
(66, 68)

7. ((This), This here) pen is mine.
(71)

8. Clumsy Mr. Tripflip survived his fall from the treetop but was a(n) ((invalid), hemisphere, wright)
(55) for several weeks.

9. Laurent (cent, (sent), scent) Vincent a postcard from Austria.
(77)

10. Shane lives in a(n) (antifreeze, (suburb), rite) of Los Angeles.
(80)

11. Does Victoria know (ware, wear, (where)) Aimee lives?
(72)

12. Vincent discovered that the ((consequence), icon, ware) of not sleeping is fatigue.
(76)

13. Circle each helping verb in this sentence: I (should) (have) (been) resting all day yesterday.
(9)

14. Circle each letter that should be capitalized below.
(6, 29)
  (d)ear (m)r. (s)treeton,

   (T)hank you for helping at (W)estfield (E)lementary (S)chool's
recent food drive. (W)e surpassed our goal by ten percent!

       (S)incerely,

       (m)s. (f)rancine (f)armer

15. Underline the two prepositional phrases in this sentence, and circle the object of each
(17, 33) preposition:

   A person born <u>on (February 29)</u> <u>in a leap (year)</u> has a birthday only every four years.

16. Circle the predicate nominative in this sentence: James Madison was the first (president) who did
(41) not wear knee breeches.

For 17–19, refer to this sentence: (Because)Americans supported the French Revolution, <u>they adopted the trousers of the revolutionaries.</u>

17. Underline the independent clause with one line.
(61)

18. Underline the dependent clause with two lines.
(61)

19. Circle the subordinating conjunction.
(61)

20. From the list below, circle the indefinite pronoun that can be either singular or plural:
(72)

several   another   (most)   many   few   no one

21. Add quotation marks to this sentence:
(69, 70)

Mr. Landis explained, "It was actually Beau Brummell who popularized trousers in England."

22. Underline each word that should be italicized in this sentence:
(73)

Treasure <u>Island</u>, a novel by Robert Louis Stevenson, remains a favorite classic.

Add correct punctuation marks to sentences 23 and 24.

23. Peter lives at 52 N. Cedar Ave., Utica, New York.
(40, 47)

24. She may decide to leave, or she may stay here.
(64)

25. Diagram this sentence in the space to the right:
(23, 25) James Madison wore long trousers.

| James Madison | wore | trousers |

long

Give after Lesson 90.

Circle the correct words to complete sentences 1–13.

1. Blood flows away from the heart through an artery; it flows toward the heart through a (vane,
(82) vain, (vein)).

2. The soldier received a special (mettle, (medal), metal) for his bravery during the war.
(85)

3. My cousin has (live, lives, (lived)) in the East all her life.
(78)

4. The 1930s (brung, (brought), bringed) a period of hardship and poverty known as the Great
(74) Depression.

5. Tweezers (was, (were)) used to pull the splinter out of Francisco's finger.
(78, 81)

6. The old horse was galloping (good, (well)) this morning.
(85)

7. Samara and Chris had a ((good), well) horseback ride through the forest.
(85)

8. Write the plural of *family*. ___families___
(13, 14)

9. Another word for loyalty is (reconcile, (allegiance), metal).
(81)

10. We might (imply, (infer), heal) from Josephine's smile that she is happy today.
(79)

11. Are you (already, (all ready)) to take your dictation test?
(83)

12. I hoped that Mr. Tripflip would (heel, (heal)) quickly.
(84)

13. Kristina is (anxious, (eager)) to chat with her best friend after school.
(78)

14. Circle the present perfect verb phrase in this sentence:
(19)

Finally, Fred (has memorized) forty-two simple prepositions.

15. Underline each prepositional phrase in this sentence, and circle the object of each preposition:
(17, 33)

Historians still argue <u>about the (cause)</u> <u>of the (Great Depression)</u>

16. Circle each letter that should be capitalized in this sentence:
(6, 29)

(i)n our history class, (m)iss (c)asey talked about the effect of the (g)reat (d)epression in the (e)ast.

17. Circle the verb in this sentence, and circle to show whether it is transitive or intransitive:
(32, 2)

(Did) you (proofread) your social studies report on the Great Depression? ((transitive), intransitive)

18. Add commas as needed to this sentence: During the Great Depression**,** factories produced more
(47, 56) than was demanded**,** and workers lost their jobs as a result.

19. Circle the nominative case pronoun in this sentence: "(They) invested their money too heavily in
(55) the stock market," Miss Casey told us.

Add quotation marks if needed to sentences 20 and 21.

20. Ernie said, **"**I am very careful with money because I lived through the Great Depression.**"**
(69, 70)

21. **"**Simple Simon**"** is a rhyme from the *Mother Goose* collection.
(70)

22. Circle the word(s) that should be italicized in this sentence:
(73)

Have you ever read the novel (Black Beauty)?

23. Insert a dash where it is needed in this sentence: Sophie finished reading *Gone with the Wind*
(77) quickly—in less than three days.

24. Add hyphens as needed in this sentence: Oops, I added one**-**fourth cup of cinnamon instead of
(86) one**-**fourth teaspoon!

25. Diagram this sentence in the space below: This was another reason for the Great Depression.
(44, 59)

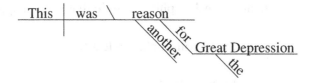

Circle the correct words to complete sentences 1–13.

1. The lost bear (past, (passed)) by the runner before lumbering back into the wilderness.
(88)

2. A person under the age of twenty-one is labeled a (miner, (minor)).
(87)

3. Some people (looks, (look)) for someone else to blame for their misery.
(78, 81)

4. The political (partys, (parties)) accused each other of leading the country in the wrong direction.
(13)

5. Some people believed that President Roosevelt was ((more), most) caring than President Hoover.
(91)

6. Is the car running (good, (well)) today?
(85)

7. The word "not" is an (adjective, (adverb)).
(82, 90)

8. The brown squirrel buried ((its), it's) acorn.
(15, 60)

9. Six-year-old Kevin has two ((loose), lose, loss) teeth.
(89)

10. Sometimes an old wooden floor will (creek, (creak)) when you walk on it.
(86)

11. Please read the story (allowed, (aloud)) so that we can all enjoy it.
(90)

12. Grandma's bicycle doesn't move; it is ((stationary), stationery).
(73)

13. One of Justin's admirable qualities is his ((humility), arrogance). He is not overly proud.
(70)

14. In the blanks below, write the four principal parts of the verb *snore*.
(16)

    (a) present tense:___snore(s)___   (b) present participle:___(is) snoring___

    (c) past tense:___snored___   (d) past participle:___(has) snored___

15. Circle each letter that should be capitalized in this sentence, and underline each word that should
(6, 20) be italicized:

    (a)unt (C)harlene asked, "(d)o you know, (c)ousin (h)arley, who took my copy of (d)avid
    (C)opperfield by (C)harles (d)ickens?"

16. Circle the appositive in this sentence: The next President after Herbert Hoover was a Democrat,
(48) (Franklin Delano Roosevelt)

17. Add commas as needed in this sentence: Jordan asked**,** "Did you know, Carey**,** that during the
(56, 65) Great Depression**,** people ridiculed President Herbert Hoover?"

18. Circle the negative in this sentence: Did (nobody) believe that Hoover was doing all he could to
(82) help Americans during the Great Depression?

Add hyphens where they are needed in sentences 19 and 20.

19. Thirty-seven cows watched a fast-moving train disappear into the night.
(86)

20. Some parents do not allow their children to watch R-rated movies.
(86)

For 21 and 22, circle to show whether the italicized word is an adjective or an adverb.

21. That was a *hard* problem. (adjective, adverb)
(27, 84)

22. The math student worked *hard* on the problem. (adjective, adverb)
(27, 84)

Diagram sentences 23–25 in the space to the right.

23. Many Americans blamed Herbert Hoover.
(23, 25)

| Americans | blamed | Herbert Hoover |

Many

24. The human suffering during the Great
(34, 44) Depression seemed limitless.

suffering | seemed \ limitless

The human   during Great Depression

the

25. That salesperson might have been working too long.
(23, 95)

salesperson | might have been working

That   long

too

Give after Lesson 100.

Circle the correct words to complete sentences 1–11.

1. The baker (peared, (pared), paired) the apples and pears before placing them in the unbaked pie
(94) crust.

2. My lost friend did not know ((whether), weather) to turn right or left.
(91)

3. Little Boy Blue has (blow, blew, (blown)) his horn several times already.
(92)

4. Can't (nobody, (anybody)) find the boy who is in charge of the sheep and cattle?
(82, 98)

5. Franklin Delano Roosevelt and his wife, Eleanor, (was, (were)) good leaders during difficult times.
(15, 78)

6. Robert, you have sneezed repeatedly; are you feeling ((well), good) today?
(85)

7. Leslie ((blew), blue) up twenty-six red balloons.
(92)

8. My (deer, (dear)) Aunt Sue baked me a cherry pie.
(93)

9. Unfortunately, our camp ((site), cite, sight) had no trees to offer shade.
(95)

10. After surgery, Mr. Tripflip was not ((allowed), aloud) to climb trees for six weeks.
(90)

11. The ((weather), whether) ((vane), vain, vein) indicates that the wind is blowing from the north.
(91, 82)

12. Circle each letter that should be capitalized in this sentence:
(6, 12)

(O)n (m)onday, (i) asked, "(W)here is the boy who looks after the sheep?"

13. Underline the prepositional phrase, and circle the object of the preposition in this sentence:
(17, 33)

The sheep are grazing <u>in the (meadow)</u>

14. Add periods as they are needed in this sentence: Little Boy Blue blew his horn at 8 a.m. daily.
(36, 40)

15. Circle the predicate nominative in this sentence:
(41)

Little Boy Blue was the sleepy young (man) under the haystack.

16. Add commas as they are needed in this sentence:
(49)

Where were you, Little Boy Blue, while the animals were escaping?

17. Circle the personal pronoun in this sentence, and circle to show whether the pronoun is first, second, or third person:
(58)

Did (you) know that, in the 1880s, schools were established for Native Americans? (1st, (2nd) 3rd person)

18. Circle the reflexive personal pronoun in this sentence:
(62)

When she returned home from school, Little Dove busied (herself) with the household chores.

For 19–21, refer to this sentence: (Although) Native Americans gained knowledge in these schools, they lost much of their tribal heritage.

19. Underline the dependent clause with one line.
(61)

20. Underline the independent clause with two lines.
(61)

21. Circle the subordinating conjunction.
(61)

22. Circle to show whether the italicized word in each sentence is an adjective or an adverb.
(44, 89)

(a) Her departure was *early*. ((adjective,) adverb) (b) She departed *early*. (adjective, (adverb))

23. Write the comparison forms for the irregular adverb *badly*.
(91)

positive _____badly_____   comparative _____worse_____   superlative _____worst_____

24. Insert a colon where it is needed in this sentence:
(94)

The cheese spread contains these ingredients**:** butter, garlic, romano cheese, and parmesan cheese.

25. Diagram the following sentence in the space below: Now, Native Americans can learn Navajo language and history at school.
(87, 95)

Circle the correct words to complete sentences 1–11.

1. Flowers that bloom year after year are called (biannuals, (perennials), semiannuals).
(96)

2. The photographer brought a (toxin, triangle, (tripod)) to support his camera.
(97)

3. A dependent clause may be connected to an independent clause by a (coordinating,
(61) (subordinating)) conjunction.

4. The sentence below is (simple, compound, (complex), compound-complex).
(99)
　　　　　The pronoun patrol apprehended me because I used the word "hisself."

5. Down the hill (come, (comes)) Jill.
(78, 79)

6. This sentence is ((active), passive) voice: Jack broke his crown.
(100)

7. The prefix (tri-, (anti-), homo-) means "against."
(65)

8. After (sometime, (some time), sometimes) had passed, Mr. Tripflip felt better.
(102)

9. *Loyalty* and (*frugality,* (*fidelity*) *patience*) have almost the same meaning.
(103)

10. *Truth* and ((*verity*) *forbearance, frugality*) have almost the same meaning.
(100)

11. Daniel and Mark do not waste money; they are (homonyms, (frugal), ultramodern).
(105)

12. Add periods as needed to this sentence: On Sunday morning, Dec. 7, 1941, the Japanese bombed
(36, 40) Pearl Harbor.

13. Add commas as needed to this sentence: Hey, Grandpa, I think Jack plastered his head with
(49, 56) vinegar and brown paper.

14. Circle the four subordinating conjunctions in this list: (since), over, (while), jump, (in order that),
(61) camera, (although), anxious

15. Add quotation marks to this sentence: After the bombing, millions of young men flocked to the
(69) military crying, "Remember Pearl Harbor!"

Add hyphens where they are needed in sentences 16 and 17.

16. Antoine treasured his paint-stained overalls.
(86)

17. Two thirds of the world's eggplant is grown in New Jersey. no hyphen (fraction is used as a noun)
(86)

18. Circle the adverb in this sentence: (Immediately), President Roosevelt declared war on Japan.
(89)

Circle the correct part of speech for the italicized word in sentences 19 and 20.

19. The manatee rolled *over*. (~~adverb~~ preposition)
(96)

20. The manatee rolled *over* me. (adverb ~~preposition~~)
(96)

Add apostrophes where they are needed in sentences 21 and 22.

21. Charlie said, "I've been talkin' to the old fisherman since six o'clock this mornin'."
(97)

22. It's amazing to me that in the year '01, there were fewer people than chickens.
(97)

23. Add a semicolon and an apostrophe where they are needed in this sentence:
(92, 98)

    Delilah's answer was correct; the longest one-syllable word is *screeched.*

24. Add a colon where it is needed in this sentence: Christie told me a curious fact: "The flag
(94) pictured on a Canadian two-dollar bill is an American flag."

25. Diagram this sentence in the space below: A dragonfly normally lives for a few weeks.
(23, 95)

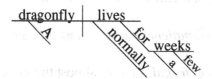

Give after Lesson 107.

Circle the correct words to complete sentences 1–9.

1. While conscientiousness and diligence are desirable character traits, (punctuality,
(107) (procrastination) perseverance) is not.

2. The giving of one's time, talents, and money is an example of ((generosity), sympathy, willpower).
(106)

3. They (was, (were)) diligent, hard-working students.
(78, 81)

4. I cannot ((conceive), concieve) of a person sailing in a bowl.
(107)

5. The prefix (*uni-* (*re-*), *poly-*) means "again."
(99)

6. A doe is a female (dear, (deer)).
(93)

7. Last night's sunset was a beautiful (site, cite, (sight)).
(95)

8. The prefix (*uni-*, *poly-* (*tri-*)) means "three."
(97)

9. Justin shares freely. He is (frugal, patient, (generous)) and unselfish.
(106)

10. Circle the helping verb in this sentence: John Scott Harrison (was) born in Indiana in 1804.
(9)

11. Circle the linking verb in this sentence: John Scott Harrison (was) the son of William Henry
(22) Harrison, the ninth President of the United States; and the father of Benjamin Harrison, the
twenty-third President.

12. Write the plural of each noun: turkey ____turkeys____ tray ____trays____
(13)
                           boss ____bosses____ puppy ____puppies____

13. Circle each letter that should be capitalized in this rhyme:
(6, 12)
           (t)hree wise men of (g)othan
           (w)ent to sea in a bowl.
           (i)f the bowl had been stronger,
           (m)y song would have been longer.

14. Circle each letter that should be capitalized in this outline, and add periods as needed:
(20)
           (i.)(f)lowers
             (a.)(a)nnuals
             (b.)(p)erennials

15. Circle the possessive pronoun in this sentence: They thought the bowl was (theirs).
(60)

16. Circle the demonstrative pronoun in this sentence: (That) was their silly mode of transportation.
(71)

17. Circle each adverb in this sentence: The three wise men of Gotham (happily) sailed (everywhere).
(84, 87)

18. Add a colon where it is needed in this sentence: Sometimes I misspell these words**:** receive,
(94) separate, etc.

19. Write the possessive form of each of these plural nouns:
(97)

turkeys _____turkeys'_____   students _____students'_____

winners _____winners'_____   mice _____mice's_____

20. Write the four principal parts of the verb *break*.
(16)

(a) present tense:_____break(s)_____   (b) present participle:_____(is) breaking_____

(c) past tense:_____broke_____   (d) past participle:_____(has) broken_____

For 21–24, refer to this sentence: <u>Three men went to sea in a bowl,</u> | but | (they didn't have much luck.)

21. Underline the first independent clause.
(37)

22. Circle the second independent clause.
(37, 61)

23. Draw a box around the coordinating conjunction.
(37, 61)

24. Diagram the sentence in the space below.
(87, 95) Three men went to sea in a bowl, but they didn't have much luck.

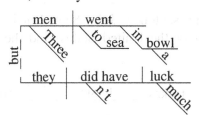

25. Diagram the following sentence in the space below: Yes, he gave me the address.
(35, 102)

Circle the correct words to complete sentences 1–10.

1. A person with allergies is aided by a group of medicines called (homophones, antihistamines,
(101) hemiplegia).

2. The poison, or toxin, of a black widow spider can be neutralized with an (antitoxin, antiseptic,
(101) hemistich).

3. The sentence below is (simple, compound, complex).
(99)

Even though it doesn't make any difference, cows are always milked from the right side,
probably because most people are right-handed.

4. The farmer (saw, seen, sawed) his mistake when he attempted to milk the cow from the left side.
(75, 78)

5. He didn't eat (anything, nothing) besides a banana before school.
(82)

6. Laurent wore a (pare, pear, pair) of shiny black shoes to the concert.
(94)

7. The prefix (*uni-*, *geo-*, *hemi-*) means "half."
(67)

8. Silver is a lustrous (metal, mettle, medal) used for coins, tableware, jewelry, etc.
(85)

9. Delay and postponement are similar to (generosity, procrastination, antitoxin).
(106, 107)

10. Josephine likes the sunshine and (blew, blue) sky in Southern California.
(92)

11. Write the four principal parts of the verb *grip*.
(16, 106)

   (a) present tense:_____grip(s)_____   (b) present participle:_____(is) gripping_____

   (c) past tense:_____gripped_____   (d) past participle:_____(has) gripped_____

12. Circle the appositive in this sentence: The pumpkin eater, Peter, had a wife but couldn't take
(48) care of her.

13. Circle each letter that should be capitalized in this sentence: hey, grandpa, why did peter put his
(6, 12) wife into a pumpkin on tuesday?

Add commas where they are needed in sentences 14 and 15.

14. Well, if Peter put his wife into a pumpkin, he could keep her from harm.
(56)

15. She would be safe, and he would be happy.
(65)

16. Circle the objective case pronoun in this sentence: She wished that he wouldn't keep her as a
(57) prisoner.

17. Circle the nominative case pronoun in this sentence: Did (he) actually lock her inside the
(56) pumpkin?

18. Circle the possessive case pronoun in this sentence: She insisted the pumpkin was not (his)
(60)

19. Use a hyphen to divide the word *president* as you would at the end of a line. __presi- dent__
(88)

20. Underline the prepositional phrase used as an adverb in this sentence, and circle the word it
(17, 95) modifies:

Most Americans (live) within fifty miles of their birthplace.

21. Add a semicolon where it is needed in this sentence: An ostrich has large eyes; they are bigger
(92) than its brain.

22. Write the possessive form of each noun or noun pair.
(97)

Keats ___Keats's___   grandparents ___grandparents'___

Scot and Debby (their dog) ___Scot and Debby's___   Mr. Fox ___Mr. Fox's___

23. Circle the interjection in this sentence: (Oh yes,) bullet-proof vests and fire escapes were both
(102) invented by women.

24. Circle each silent letter in these words: ma(t)ch   wa(l)k   num(b)   (w)rist   (k)new
(103, 104)

25. Diagram this sentence: Peter was poor but innovative.
(23, 44)

Circle the simple subject and underline the simple predicate in each sentence.

1. (Ice) melts.

2. (Water) changes from solid to liquid.

3. (Water) evaporates.

4. (Water) becomes vapor, a gas.

5. The water (molecules) remain the same.

6. (Scientists) write H_2O.

7. Our (bodies) need water.

8. Did (you) drink your water?

9. (We) need eight glasses daily.

10. Is the (well) dry?

11. (We) must conserve water.

12. Have (you) seen Niagara Falls?

13. (Water) is heavy.

14. A (pint) weighs about a pound.

15. A (gallon) weighs about eight pounds.

16. Can (you) swim?

17. The (water) holds you up.

18. Our (bodies) can float.

19. (Swimming) strengthens our muscles.

20. (Mr. Pemberton) swam the English Channel.

Write a capital letter on each letter that should be capitalized in these sentences.

1. The highest elevation in the United States is Mount McKinley, Alaska, at 20,320 feet.

2. The lowest elevation in the United States is in Death Valley, California, at 282 feet below sea level.

3. The deepest lake in the U.S. is Crater Lake in Oregon.

4. The highest waterfall in North America is Yosemite Falls in Yosemite, California.

5. Have you ever seen the Empire State Building in New York City?

6. I read the poem "The Road Not Taken" by Robert Frost.

7. Robert attends Charles E. Gidley School in El Monte, California.

8. Mrs. Rivas teaches at Mercer College in New Jersey.

9. The United States is half the size of Russia and slightly smaller than China.

10. The Mississippi River flows into the Gulf of Mexico.

11. Have you ever swum in the Pacific Ocean?

12. Peggy and Ed dive deep in the Atlantic Ocean.

13. A building called the Sears Tower stands 1454 feet tall in Chicago, Illinois.

14. Our largest national park, Wrangell-St. Elias, is located in Alaska.

15. The Appalachian Mountains have lush green forests.

16. The Curtises stayed in a town called Big Bear on Saturday night.

17. Next Tuesday, February 20, Mr. Grouch will fly to a city in Iowa called Des Moines.

18. Have you seen the famous Golden Gate Bridge in San Francisco, California?

Underline the entire verb phrase in each sentence.

1. By 1929, the Great Depression <u>had come</u> to the United States.

2. It <u>had spread</u> to Europe as well.

3. Many German workers <u>had lost</u> their jobs.

4. Germans <u>were looking</u> for a strong leader.

5. Hitler <u>was making</u> himself the absolute dictator.

6. Germans <u>should have looked</u> elsewhere for a leader.

7. Hitler <u>was blaming</u> Germany's problems on the Jews.

8. His systematic hatred and persecution of the Jews <u>would lead</u> to one of the most horrendous periods of history.

9. In 1938, Hitler <u>was marching</u> to conquer the world.

10. By April 1940, the Germans <u>had conquered</u> Denmark and Norway.

11. Hitler <u>could have dominated</u> all of Europe.

12. However, the British <u>would</u> not <u>surrender</u>.

13. Most Americans <u>were sympathizing</u> with Britain's lonely fight.

14. <u>Should</u> America <u>have stayed</u> out of the war?

15. President Franklin D. Roosevelt <u>was saying</u> this:

16. "America <u>must become</u> the arsenal of democracy."

17. Americans <u>might have remained</u> isolationists.

18. Meanwhile, the Japanese <u>had been invading</u> China.

19. The Japanese <u>had formed</u> an alliance with Germany.

20. On December 7, 1941, American soldiers at Pearl Harbor <u>could see</u> the red circles on the Japanese planes.

21. Your grandfather or great grandfather <u>might have fought</u> in World War II.

22. We <u>shall remember</u> the brave veterans, and we <u>shall honor</u> them always.

Silly Story #1

(After Lesson 10)

Instructions to Teacher   Have the student number a blank, lined piece of paper from 1 to 24. Ask him or her to write an example of the indicated part of speech beside each number. Proceed slowly, and frequently question the student to be sure he or she has written a correct example of the part of speech you have requested for each blank space in the story.

After the list has been completed, give the student a copy of "Harvest Stew." Ask him or her to write each word from the list in the blank space with the corresponding number. Then ask the student to read the story aloud.

Harvest Stew   Two friends, (1) _proper noun (person)_ and (2) _proper noun (person)_,

who live in (3) _proper noun (place)_ , made a harvest stew for their

(4) _feminine noun_ . First they placed some (5) _concrete plural noun_

and (6) _concrete plural noun_ in the pot. They added a dash of

(7) _concrete singular noun —neuter gender_ and water, and they turned on the heat to

(8) _number_ degrees Fahrenheit. Delighted and excited,

they (9) _past tense action verb_ and (10) _past tense action verb_ . They said,

"We are a (11) _collective noun_ !"

When the stew began to boil, they tossed in a

(12) _concrete singular noun_ and a (13) _concrete, singular compound noun_ for flavor.

They asked their friend, (14) _proper noun (person)_ , to taste it. Then

they chopped up some (15) _concrete plural noun_ and diced a

(16) _concrete singular noun_ for good measure.

A (17) _masculine noun_ watched them from the window.

When he smelled the aroma, he began to (18) _present tense action verb_ .

The cooks ignored him and added (19) _____number_____ more

(20)_concrete plural noun_ to the pot for color.

The stew tasted so delicious, the cooks shared it with all

the (21)_plural noun indefinite gender_ in the neighborhood. Afterward, they

felt full of (22) _abstract singular noun_ and (23)_abstract singular noun_.

They happily gave the leftovers to (24)_proper noun (person)_.

Write a capital letter over each letter that should be capitalized in these sentences.

1. Winston Churchill declared, "We shall defend our island home . . . ."

2. Have you read <u>The Magic Bicycle</u> by John Bibee?

3. He also wrote <u>The Only Game in Town</u>.

4. David and Karen Mains wrote <u>Tales of the Kingdom</u>.

5. They also wrote <u>Tales of the Resistance</u>.

6. I. Stones
   A. Where they are found
   B. What they contain

7. II. Crystals
   A. How they are formed
   B. The story of granite

8. Grandma reminded us, "A pint is a pound the world around."

9. Oscar missed the school bus and forgot his Tuesday homework, but at the end of the day he sighed, "All's well that ends well."

10. Ruth and David Elliott wrote <u>The Richest Kid in the Poor House</u>.

11. President Dwight D. Eisenhower said, "The clearest way to show what the rule of law means to us in everyday life is to recall what has happened when there is no rule of law."

12. "Why did the Roman Empire fall?" asked Miss Casey.

13. In 1776, Thomas Paine said, "What we obtain too cheap, we esteem too lightly."

14. "The Germans should conquer and rule the world," Hitler told his people.

15. Anne Frank wrote, "I can feel the suffering of millions . . . ."

16. Edmund Burke said, "The only thing necessary for the triumph of evil is for good men to do nothing."

Write a capital letter over each letter that should be capitalized in these sentences.

1. Mr. and Mrs. **P**érez teach **S**panish at **P**ortantorchas **S**chool in **C**osta **R**ica.

2. **S**omeday you might enjoy taking **P**rofessor **M**hunzi's **A**frican **A**merican history class.

3. **D**oes **G**randpa speak **F**rench?

4. Mrs. **L**ópez excels in math and physics.

5. **I**s your father learning to speak **E**nglish?

6. **I** asked **D**ad to have lunch with me.

7. **W**hen will **R**abbi **F**eingold arrive?

8. **D**id **U**ncle **B**ill play the trumpet last night?

9. **I** believe **D**r. **Y**u is delivering a baby right now.

10. **H**ave you spoken with **S**ergeant **P**alusso or **C**aptain **R**ice?

11. **I** helped **M**om clean the house and wash the cars.

12. **H**ave you helped your mother lately?

13. **H**ave you seen **G**randma **M**oses's paintings?

14. **M**y grandfather and **I** served meals to the homeless at **B**ethany **C**hurch in **L**ittle **R**ock, **A**rkansas.

15. **D**o **A**unt **M**argaret and **U**ncle **C**harles play the **F**rench horn?

16. Mrs. **C**ordasco cooks delicious **I**talian food.

17. **D**id **F**ather spend the winter in **B**ismarck, **N**orth **D**akota?

18. **J**ustin and **T**revor fixed **M**exican food for their brother **J**ared.

19. **J**ames is studying biology, music, and **R**ussian history.

20. **V**ice **P**resident **I**shigaki was always punctual.

Silly Story #2
(After Lesson 27)

Instructions to Teacher   Have the student number a blank, lined piece of paper from 1 to 26. Ask him or her to write an example of the indicated part of speech beside each number. Proceed slowly, and frequently question the student to be sure he or she has written a correct example of the part of speech you have requested for each blank space in the story.

After the list has been completed, give the student a copy of "Holiday Decor." Ask him or her to write each word from the list in the blank space with the corresponding number. Then ask the student to read the story aloud.

Holiday Decor   (1)_proper noun (person)_ and (2)_proper noun (person)_ decided to

decorate for the holiday party of the (3)_collective noun_ .

"First of all," they agreed, "we (4)_future tense action verb_ and we

(5)_future tense action verb_ before we start." After (6)_present participle form of a verb_ and

(7)_present participle form of a verb_ for several hours, they had (8)_past participle form of a verb_

and (9)_past participle form of a verb_ , and realized they had been

procrastinating. So they started to work without wasting any

more time.

They began decorating with (10)_descriptive adjective_ lights

and (11)_descriptive adjective_ balloons (12)_preposition_ the

fireplace. They hung (13)_proper possessive noun (person)_ socks (14)_preposition_

a (15)_concrete singular noun_ for added (16)_abstract singular noun_ .

When they had finished, there were (17)_descriptive adjective_ ,

(18)_descriptive adjective_ decorations everywhere— (19)__preposition__

the tables, (20)_____preposition_____ the walls, (21)_____preposition_____ the

doors, (22)_____preposition_____ the windows, (23)_____preposition_____

the floors, and (24)_____preposition_____ the ceilings. The decorators

(25)____past tense linking verb (for a plural subject)____ (26)____descriptive adjective____ . It was a lovely sight.

More Practice Lesson 28

Underline each adjective in these sentences.

1. <u>A</u> channel is <u>a deep</u>, <u>narrow</u> body of water connecting <u>two larger</u> bodies of water.

2. <u>The Polstein's</u> son lives at <u>the</u> delta—<u>a flat</u>, <u>sandy</u> area at <u>the</u> mouth of <u>the</u> river.

3. <u>Most</u> people live on plains, which are <u>flat</u>, <u>level</u> areas of land.

4. <u>Some</u> people live in <u>a</u> canyon, <u>a narrow</u> valley with <u>steep</u> sides.

5. <u>A</u> harbor is <u>a sheltered</u>, <u>safe</u> place for ships to anchor.

6. <u>This</u> ship will enter <u>that</u> bay on <u>its final</u> voyage.

7. <u>A</u> sound is <u>a wide</u> channel linking <u>two large</u> bodies of water.

8. <u>Many</u> tourists enjoy <u>beautiful</u> Puget Sound in <u>the</u> Northwest.

9. <u>The adventurous</u> explorer wanted to climb <u>the highest</u> mountain in <u>the</u> world.

10. <u>Europe's important</u> waterway is <u>the busy</u> Rhine River.

11. <u>The</u> altitude of <u>magnificent</u> Mt. Everest is <u>twenty-nine thousand twenty-eight</u> feet.

12. <u>Some mountain</u> ranges form <u>a</u> boundary between <u>two</u> countries.

13. <u>The mountainous</u> continent of Asia has <u>the most</u> people.

14. Antarctica is <u>a</u> continent with <u>no native human</u> population.

15. <u>The</u> circumference of <u>the</u> earth is <u>twenty-five thousand</u> miles.

16. <u>The earth's</u> diameter is <u>eight thousand</u> miles.

17. <u>The hot</u>, <u>humid rain</u> forests in <u>tropical</u> regions have <u>tall</u> trees and <u>heavy</u> vines.

18. In <u>hot</u>, <u>savanna</u> regions, <u>some</u> trees and <u>tall</u>, <u>tough</u> grasses grow.

Underline every capital letter that does not belong in these sentences.

1. I saw a <u>R</u>hinoceros, a <u>H</u>ippopotamus, and an African <u>E</u>lephant at the San Diego Zoo.

2. Mrs. Wellbaum grows <u>P</u>ecans and English <u>W</u>alnuts.

3. She has also planted <u>D</u>aisies, <u>G</u>eraniums, and African <u>V</u>iolets.

4. Do you prefer German <u>C</u>hocolate <u>C</u>ake or <u>F</u>udge <u>B</u>rownies?

5. The students played <u>S</u>occer, <u>V</u>olleyball, and <u>T</u>ennis in gym class.

6. Gretchen was studying <u>M</u>ath, <u>B</u>iology, and <u>G</u>eology when she caught the <u>C</u>hicken <u>P</u>ox.

7. I like <u>T</u>acos, <u>B</u>urritos, and <u>E</u>nchiladas, but he prefers Chinese <u>F</u>ood.

8. In the <u>S</u>pring, I will plant Italian <u>S</u>quash, <u>T</u>omatoes, and <u>C</u>ucumbers.

9. We pick our <u>A</u>pricots, <u>P</u>eaches, and <u>P</u>lums in the <u>S</u>ummer.

10. Next <u>F</u>all, the Halls will return to the East Coast.

11. During the <u>W</u>inter, perhaps the Steinbrons will visit the West Coast.

12. Mr. Zee is recovering from a bad case of <u>T</u>onsillitis.

13. Last <u>F</u>all, he was tested for illnesses such as <u>M</u>alaria, <u>T</u>uberculosis, and <u>H</u>epatitis.

14. For entertainment, he plays <u>C</u>harades and does <u>C</u>rossword <u>P</u>uzzles.

15. He longs for his favorite foods: <u>F</u>ried <u>R</u>ice, <u>S</u>paghetti, and <u>N</u>achos with French <u>P</u>eas.

16. I bought some tasty Danish <u>P</u>astries at a bakery in a <u>T</u>own called Solvang.

For 1–5, complete the partially constructed sentence diagram.

1. King Tut and Queen Hatshepsut lived in ancient Egypt.

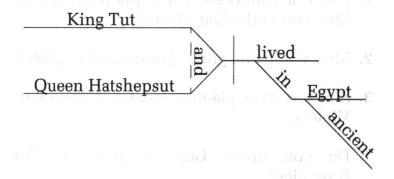

2. Treasure, weapons, and food filled Egyptian tombs.

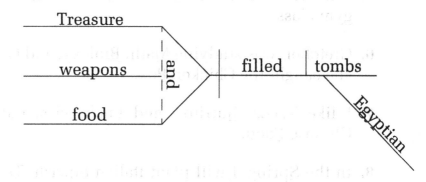

3. Egyptians hammered and dragged the huge, rough stone blocks.

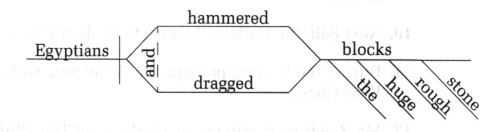

4. The Phoenicians sailed the Mediterranean, traded their goods, and developed an alphabet.

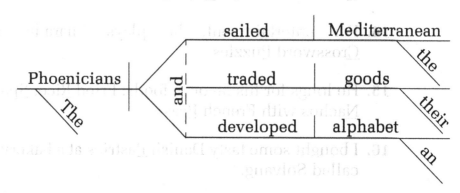

5. The Hittites conquered and oppressed other ancient kingdoms.

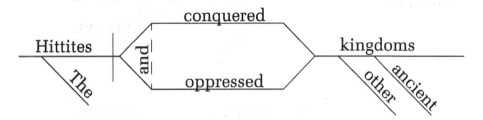

On a separate piece of paper, diagram sentences 6–13.

6. Mountains, deserts, and rivers divide the country of India.

7. People in ancient India counted, measured, and wrote.

8. Indian farmers and family groups plowed, planted, and harvested.

9. Hindu temples and shrines represent and honor the many Hindu gods.

10. Ancient Indians invented chess, polo, and playing cards.

11. The people rode camels, oxen, and elephants.

12. Cattle and other animals received special treatment.

13. India's flag features a gold stripe and a green stripe.

6.

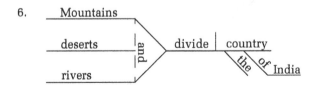

7.

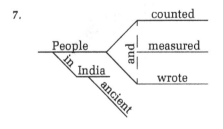

8.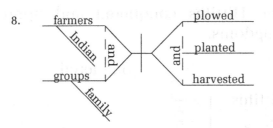

9.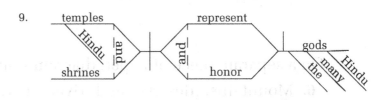

10.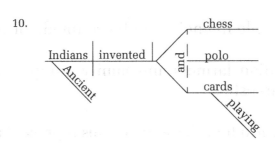

11.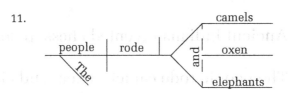

12.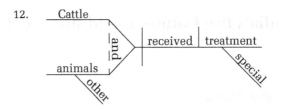

13.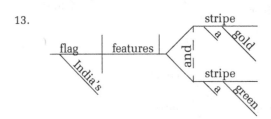

For 1 and 2, add periods where they are needed in the following outlines.

1. I. Geography facts
    A. Hemispheres
    B. Continents
    C. Oceans

2. II. Landforms
    A. Plains
    B. Mountains
    C. Plateaus

For sentences 3–12, add periods where they are needed.

3. Richard M. Nixon became president in 1969.

4. Lyndon B. Johnson became president after John F. Kennedy was assassinated in 1963.

5. Choose your friends carefully.

6. Think before you speak.

7. She dated her letter Sun., Nov. 4, 2001.

8. My phone bill was over $95.00 (ninety-five dollars) last month!

9. Gen. Robert E. Lee said to his son, "Never do a wrong thing to make a friend or keep one."

10. Mail this package to:

Ms. Petunia U. Blossom
5722 W. Magnolia Rd.
Bloomsville, Utah 84490

11. She likes baseball, basketball, football, etc., but she doesn't like hockey.

12. Scot rarely goes to bed before 11 p.m.

For 13–15, write the months of the year whose names we do not abbreviate.

13.   May   **14.**   June   **15.**   July

For 16–19, use decimal points and numerals to write these numbers in the blanks.

16. $20.43   twenty dollars and forty-three cents

17.   16.52   sixteen and fifty-two hundredths

18.   10.4   ten and four tenths

19. $3.50   three dollars and fifty cents

Place commas wherever they are needed in these sentences.

1. On June 28, 1914, a Serbian assassinated the heir to the Austrian throne.

2. World War I began on July 28, 1914, when Austria declared war on Serbia.

3. Russia mobilized for conflict on July 30, 1914.

4. On August 1, 1914, Germany declared war on Russia.

5. Germany declared war on France on August 3. no commas needed

6. Germany, Austria-Hungary, and Italy made up the Triple Alliance.

7. The Triple Entente included Great Britain, France, and Russia.

8. On April 6, 1917, Congress declared war on Germany.

9. Private organizations like the Red Cross, the YMCA, the Salvation Army, the Knights of Columbus, and the Jewish Welfare Board helped in the war effort.

10. On November 11, 1918, in Compiègne, France, representatives of the Allies, as well as those of Germany, signed an armistice to end the war.

11. The Peace Conference convened January 18, 1919, at a palace called Versailles.

12. Versailles is located outside of Paris, France.

13. President Woodrow Wilson collapsed after delivering a speech in Pueblo, Colorado, on September 25, 1919.

For 14–16, place commas where they are needed in these addresses.

14. 11147 Bunbury Street, Saint Louis, Missouri

15. 270 Alta Vista Drive, Tallahassee, Florida

16. 4921 Cedar Avenue, Topeka, Kansas

17. 30 Pine Street, Steamboat Springs, Colorado

Instructions to Teacher   Have the student number a blank, lined piece of paper from 1 to 30. Ask him or her to write an example of the indicated part of speech beside each number. Proceed slowly, and frequently question the student to be sure he or she has written a correct example of the part of speech you have requested for each blank space in the story.

After the list has been completed, give the student a copy of "A Love Story." Ask him or her to write each word from the list in the blank space with the corresponding number. Then ask the student to read the story aloud.

A Love Story   (1) proper noun (feminine) could hardly wait until Valentine's Day. She loved Brock Lee and planned a (2) descriptive adjective surprise for him. She thought, "Brock Lee is (3) comparative adjective and (4) comparative adjective than any other man I know. In fact, he is the (5) superlative adjective man in the whole world."

To be nice, she would first (6) present tense transitive verb and (7) present tense transitive verb him. Perhaps she would give him an unusual (8) descriptive adjective (9) concrete singular noun to prove her (10) abstract singular noun for him.

She began searching for the perfect gift. She looked (11) preposition stores, (12) preposition malls, (13) preposition catalogs, and under every single (14) concrete singular noun and (15) concrete singular noun . Finally, she decided to give him a (16) concrete singular noun and two (17) concrete plural noun .

After wrapping this (18) <u>superlative adjective</u> of presents, she

called Brock Lee on the telephone. When he said hello, she

(19) <u>past tense action verb (intransitive)</u> (20) <u>coordinating conjunction</u> (21) <u>past tense action verb (intransitive)</u>.

She could hardly speak.

Finally, she stammered, "Brock, I would like to invite you

to (22) <u>proper noun (place)</u> for dinner. I have a (23) <u>descriptive adjective</u>

present for you. You are the (24) <u>superlative adjective</u> in the

world. You are (25) <u>comparative adjective</u> than my father. I love

you more than (26) <u>concrete plural noun</u> or (27) <u>concrete plural noun</u>.

All I have to do is think about you and my heart is full of

(28) <u>abstract singular noun</u>."

There was a long, (29) <u>descriptive adjective</u> pause. Then a

strange man said in a (30) <u>descriptive adjective</u> voice, "I'm sorry,

but you must have the wrong number."

Place commas where they are needed in these sentences.

1. Joshua, where are you going?

2. Christina, I need your help!

3. Are you ready for spaghetti, Freddy?

4. Why, Margarita, did you bring your dog to school?

5. American businessman Henry Ford brought the country its first affordable car, the Model T.

6. The Model T came in one color, black.

7. My next door neighbor, a collector of antique cars, is restoring a Model T in his garage.

8. He won't paint it green, my favorite color, even though his wife, Betty, and I think it would look snazzy.

9. Emily Ishigaki, President, shared some interesting facts with the school board.

10. Mr. Seymour, the Superintendent, encouraged the teachers.

11. I believe Miss Ngo, Class Treasurer, should collect the money.

12. The authors included Herbert Zamora, Ph.D., and Mauricio Zelaya, D.D.S.

13. Patricia Childress, R.N., works at City of Hope in Duarte, California.

14. Yuan Chen, D.D.S., pulled my tooth.

15. Gloria Quigley, M.D., prescribed the antibiotics.

16. I see that Freddy Rivas, M.Div., is your new pastor.

17. Our superintendent, James Dawson, Ed.D., is quite a guy.

18. Allison, are you trying to be punctual?

19. Did you call me last night, Henry?

20. I think, dear cousin, that you need a plumber.

Place commas where they are needed in 1–12.

1. Dear Kerry,

   Please feed Snooper.

         Love,

         Mom

2. Hi Mom,

   I fed Snooper.

         Love,

         Kerry

3. Hey Joe,

   Please wait for me after school today.

         Your friend,

         Moe

4. The index listed "Webster, Noah" on page 320.

5. Under the *p*'s, I found the name "Pizarro, Francisco."

6. According to the index, "Revere, Paul" can be found on page 227.

7. I wrote "Hake, Danielle" because it asked for last name first.

8. My friend wrote "Placencia, Betty."

9. Dear Grandpa,

   My e-mail address has changed to pedro@quickmail.com.

         Your grandson,

         Pedro

10. Dear Pedro,

    Thanks for sending me your new address. I hope you're enjoying school.

          Love,

          Grandpa

11. Dear Friends,

    Thank you for the surprise party!

          Gratefully,

          Bernardo

12. Dear Mrs. Villalobos,

    I'm sorry you are sick. My prayers are with you.

          Sincerely,

          Docker Busick

Place commas where they are needed in these sentences.

1. Abraham Lincoln, we remember, did not let his childhood poverty and hardships deprive him of a successful life.

2. Through diligence and integrity, we recall, he became a respected lawyer and statesman.

3. No, he never allowed the bitterness of the Civil War to make him a bitter man.

4. Yes, he was determined to stand for what he believed was right.

5. Lincoln, I have heard, was known for his wit and his funny stories.

6. His sense of humor, I think, saw him through the dark trials of a long Civil War.

7. Lincoln never lost contact with the common people, even after he became famous.

8. Despite his busy schedule, he always found time to listen to all who came to seek his aid.

9. With unyielding persistence, Lincoln guided the nation through crisis.

10. No President, with the possible exception of George Washington, is held dearer in the hearts of the American people.

11. Abraham Lincoln illustrates better than perhaps any other hero the qualities that have made America great.
    no comma needed

12. Certainly, his integrity and kindness toward all people represent American values.

13. In addition, his courage and determination display the American tradition.

14. Therefore, we hold the memory of Abraham Lincoln in high esteem.

15. He is, without doubt, a true hero.

Underline the dependent clause in each sentence, and star the subordinating conjunction.

1. *Although George Washington Carver was born into slavery, he became one of the world's greatest contributors to agriculture.

2. I have heard *that he also sang and played the organ.

3. *When he was very young, George was keenly interested in plants.

4. *While he was still a boy, people nicknamed him "the plant doctor."

5. *After he graduated from high school, he enrolled at Simpson College in Iowa.

6. He cooked, took in laundry, and worked as a janitor *so that he could pay his college expenses.

7. In the 1890s, Iowa State Agricultural College honored him *because he had collected 20,000 species of fungi.

8. *Even though he had a promising career at Iowa State, he gave it up to help black students in the South.

9. He joined the Tuskegee Institute *because he wanted to improve southern agriculture.

10. *Wherever he went, he taught how to improve farming methods and conserve natural resources.

11. *Whenever someone needed him, he was there.

12. *While cotton was the major crop of the South, it seriously depleted the soil.

13. Peanuts would help nourish the soil *if they became a profitable crop.

14. He hoped *that he could think of more ways to use peanuts.

15. *After Carver discovered three hundred uses for the peanut, farmers began planting more peanuts.

16. Peanuts became more and more popular *until they were one of the most important cash crops in the South.

17. *Though Professor Carver became world famous for his research, he led a modest and quiet life.

18. *While Carver had achieved unquestioned greatness, he remained a humble servant throughout his life.

19. I understand *that he also taught Sunday school.

20. People recognized *that his chief desire was to serve humanity.

Place commas where they are needed in these sentences.

1. Are you aware that half the states in the U.S. have Native American names? no comma needed

2. Hiawatha was a peace-loving, influential Mohawk chief who wanted to end tribal wars.

3. Pilgrims and Native Americans worked together to survive the long, cold, cruel New England winters.

4. Because he taught the Pilgrims many things about wilderness living, Samoset became a friend of the Pilgrims.

5. I understand that he introduced the Pilgrims to Massasoit, Chief of the Wampanoag people.

6. After they signed a treaty with the Pilgrims, the Wampanoag shared the first Thanksgiving with them.

7. Tecumseh was a clever, courageous Shawnee chief.

8. As soon as he had united other tribes, he led them against the U.S. in the War of 1812.

9. Since Sequoyah had a genius for language, he devised a written alphabet of 86 characters for the Cherokees.

10. Because they had an alphabet, the Cherokees published their own books and newspapers.

11. The beautiful, forested Sequoia National Park and the magnificent Sequoia tree are named after this famous, ingenious Native American.

12. Sacajawea was a strong, adventurous Shoshone woman who guided the Lewis and Clark expedition across the West.

13. Before General Custer knew what was happening, Sitting Bull was attacking his army.

14. If Crazy Horse had not fought in the battle, the Sioux might not have won the war.

15. Black Hawk didn't know that his great-grandson would be Jim Thorpe, one of the greatest athletes in history.

Place commas where they are needed in these sentences.

1. General Robert E. Lee told his son, "Do not appear to others what you are not."

2. He also said, "Deal kindly but firmly with all your classmates."

3. Will Rogers said, "I never met a man I didn't like."

4. "Labor to keep alive... that little spark of celestial fire called conscience," said George Washington.

5. "If you stand for nothing, you'll fall for anything," Mom always said.

6. Confucius said, "Virtue is not left to stand alone."

7. He continued, "He who practices it will have neighbors."

8. Virtue is goodness, and its opposite is vice.

9. Greed is a vice, but self-discipline is a virtue.

10. Be kind to animals, for they depend on us.

11. We can have virtues, or we can have vices.

12. The woman was poor, yet she gave her last few cents.

13. He did not lie, nor did he cheat.

14. He told the truth, for he had integrity.

15. If you are always honest, people will trust you.

16. Friends will respect you if you admit a mistake.
    no comma needed

17. Dad says that we should be considerate of others.
    no comma needed

18. We can try to be virtuous, but we will never be perfect.

19. David said, "Becky, there are lots of ways to help out."

20. Becky was free that day, so she cheerfully volunteered.

Place quotation marks where they are needed in these sentences.

1. Benjamin Franklin said, "A good conscience is a continual Christmas."

2. "I cannot live without books," said Thomas Jefferson to John Adams.

3. "Some books are to be tasted," said Francis Bacon, "others to be swallowed, and some few to be chewed and digested."

4. The following words were written by British author Samuel Butler: "Books are like imprisoned souls till someone takes them down from a shelf and frees them."

5. Theodore Roosevelt said, "Books are almost as individual as friends."

6. "Friendship," said Thomas Fuller, "is not to be bought."

7. "Friendships multiply joys and divide griefs," said H. G. Bohn.

8. Edward Young said, "Procrastination is the thief of time."

9. "Never put off till tomorrow what you can do today," Lord Chesterfield told his son.

10. Aunt Delanah reminded us about the importance of good study skills. (no quotation marks needed)

11. Hesiod lived in Greece approximately 2800 years ago. "Diligence increaseth the fruit of toil," he wrote in the eighth century B.C.

12. "Life is a long lesson in humility," wrote James Barrie in 1891.

13. Sharia's mother asked her to be a good example for her little sister. (no quotation marks needed)

14. "It is hard to be high and humble," wrote Thomas Fuller in 1732.

15. "I worked hard for that *A*," said Johnna.

For 1–16, place quotation marks where they are needed in the following dialogues.

From Little Women by Louisa May Alcott:

1. "Army shoes, best to be had," cried Jo.

2. "Some handkerchiefs, all hemmed," said Beth.

3. "I'll get a little bottle of cologne. She likes it, and it won't cost much, so I'll have some left to buy my pencils," added Amy.

4. "How will we give the things?" asked Meg.

From *The Swiss Family Robinson* by Johann Wyss:

5. "What? Ho! are they really coconuts?" cried Ernest. "Do let me take them again, Mother, do let me look at them."

6. "No, thank you," replied my wife, with a smile. "I have no wish to see you again overburdened."

7. "Oh, but I have only to throw away these sticks, which are of no use, and then I can easily carry them."

8. "Worse and worse," said Fritz. "I have a particular regard for those heavy, useless sticks. Did you ever hear of sugar cane?"

From *The Adventures of Tom Sawyer* by Mark Twain:

9. "What is it!" exclaimed Joe, under his breath.

10. "I wonder," said Tom in a whisper.

11. "'Tain't thunder," said Huckleberry, in an awed tone, "because thunder—"

12. "Hark!" said Tom. "Listen—don't talk."

From *Alice in Wonderland* by Lewis Carroll:

13. "Living backwards!" Alice repeated in great astonishment. "I never heard of such a thing."

14. "—but there's one great advantage in it, that one's memory works both ways."

15. "I'm sure *mine* only works one way," Alice remarked. "I can't remember things before they happen."

16. "It's a poor sort of memory that only works backwards," the Queen remarked.

(continued)

For 17–30, enclose titles of short literary works and songs in quotation marks.

17. Oliver Wendell Holmes wrote a poem called "The Chambered Nautilus."

18. Charles Finney, an early American revivalist, preached a sermon entitled "Selfishness."

19. Josh Billings (1818-1885) wrote a humorous essay called "The Bumblebee."

20. We read Nathaniel Hawthorne's short story "The Great Carbuncle."

21. This interesting article, called "How to Clean Your Windows," came from Sunday's newspaper.

22. Marco wrote an editorial for the newspaper and titled it "Experimental Educational Reform."

23. "A Listening Heart" is the name of Jayne's poem about friendship.

24. "Dog Heroes" is the name of the magazine article that sparked my interest.

25. For his history class, John wrote an essay called "The Hydrogen Bomb."

26. For his English class, James wrote a fictional story and titled it "The Grandfather Clock."

27. Professor Gallop gave a lecture entitled "Who's Afraid of the Big Square Root?"

28. "Jeannie with the Light Brown Hair" was written by Stephen Foster in 1854.

29. Francis Bacon (1561-1626), an English philosopher, scientist, and writer, wrote an essay called "On Revenge."

30. Shakespeare's poem "When Icicles Hang by the Wall" was a favorite in Mrs. McPhail's class.

Silly Story #4
(After Lesson 72)

Instructions to Teacher Have the student number a blank, lined piece of paper from 1 to 26. Ask him or her to write an example of the indicated part of speech beside each number. Proceed slowly, and frequently question the student to be sure he or she has written a correct example of the part of speech you have requested for each blank space in the story.

After the list has been completed, give the student a copy of "Planting a Garden." Ask him or her to write each word from the list in the blank space with the corresponding number. Then ask the student to read the story aloud.

Planting a Garden Spring always gave (1) ___proper noun (person; masculine)___ the urge to plant a

garden. This year, (2) ___abstract noun___ and (3) ___abstract noun___

filled his head along with thoughts of having the

(4) ___superlative adjective___ garden of all the neighbors in

(5) ___noun (place)___ . "My (6) ___descriptive adjective___ garden will be

(7) ___comparative adjective___ than (8) ___possessive pronoun___ , (9) ___possessive pronoun___ , or

(10) ___possessive pronoun___ ," he thought.

In preparation, he (11) ___past tense transitive verb___ the soil while

eyeing the neighbors. He wondered if (12) ___proper noun (person; feminine)___

and (13) ___proper noun (person; masculine)___ were spying on him. He would

outdo (14) ___nominative case personal pronoun (feminine)___ and (15) ___nominative case personal pronoun (masculine)___ .

After (16) ___present participle form of verb___ and (17) ___present participle form of verb___ for

several hours, he began planting. First, he planted two

(18) ___concrete noun, plural___ . He hummed as he planted a row of

(19) _adjective (number)_ (20) _concrete noun, plural_ . In a very deep hole, he placed a (21) _concrete noun, singular_ and surrounded it with (22) _descriptive adjective_ marigolds. Next, he covered the entire garden with his (23) _superlative adjective_ mixture of fertilizer made from old (24) _concrete noun, plural_ and (25) _concrete noun, plural_ .

Finally, he sat down and waited for his garden to grow, satisfied that no one else would have (26) _comparative adjective_ results than he.

Underline all words that should be italicized in print.

1. Mom's favorite movie is <u>The Sound of Music</u>.

2. Uncle Charles reads <u>The New York Times</u> newspaper every morning.

3. Have you seen the musical drama called <u>Annie</u>?

4. Caleb listens to a music CD entitled <u>The Lost Boys</u>.

5. Have you read the novel <u>Moby Dick</u> by Herman Melville?

6. While in the Navy, Rick served on the aircraft carrier U.S.S. <u>Constitution</u>.

7. David named his airplane the <u>Pelican II</u>.

8. If you visit the Louvre in Paris, you might see Rembrandt's painting called <u>Bathsheba</u>.

9. Rembrandt also painted <u>The Jewish Bride</u>, which you can see in a museum in Amsterdam.

10. My brother doesn't like opera, but we went to see <u>The Magic Flute</u> anyway.

11. Please use the word <u>dilemma</u> in a sentence.

12. In 1915, the Germans attacked a large British luxury ship, the <u>Lusitania</u>, and sank it.

13. Its scientific name is <u>corvus brachyrhynchos</u>, but we usually call it a crow.

14. In 1848, Karl Marx published a book called <u>The Communist Manifesto</u>.

15. We learned today what the German word <u>gemütlichkeit</u> means. (ge-MOOT-likh-ite: "Warm friendliness, congeniality.")

16. Columbus sailed to the new world in a ship called the <u>Santa Maria</u>.

More Practice Lesson 74

Complete this irregular verb chart by writing the past and past participle forms of each verb.

VERB	PAST	PAST PARTICIPLE
1. beat	beat	(has) beaten
2. bite	bit	(has) bitten
3. bring	brought	(has) brought
4. build	built	(has) built
5. burst	burst	(has) burst
6. buy	bought	(has) bought
7. catch	caught	(has) caught
8. come	came	(has) come
9. cost	cost	(has) cost
10. dive	dove or dived	(has) dived
11. drag	dragged	(has) dragged
12. draw	drew	(has) drawn
13. drown	drowned	(has) drowned
14. drive	drove	(has) driven
15. eat	ate	(has) eaten
16. fall	fell	(has) fallen
17. feel	felt	(has) felt
18. fight	fought	(has) fought
19. find	found	(has) found
20. flee	fled	(has) fled
21. fly	flew	(has) flown
22. forget	forgot	(has) forgotten
23. forgive	forgave	(has) forgiven

Write the correct verb form for each sentence.

1. Yesterday the Blues **beat** the Reds in ping pong.

2. The Blues have **beaten** them in every tournament.

3. For yesterday's picnic, I **brought** sandwiches.

4. I have always **brought** sandwiches.

5. Last year they **built** a new house.

6. They have **built** two houses.

7. Tom **bought** Christina a ring.

8. He has **bought** a beautiful one.

9. Steve **caught** a cold.

10. I think he has **caught** a nasty one.

11. John **came** home early.

12. He has **come** home to rest.

13. Yesterday bananas **cost** 49¢ a pound.

14. They have **cost** more in the past.

15. Miss Muffett **dove (or dived)** into the lake. (Either is correct.)

16. She has **dived** often.

17. Kurt **drew** a picture.

18. He has **drawn** several.

19. Daniel **drove** around the block.

20. He has **driven** for ten years.

21. A branch **fell** out of the tree.

22. Branches have **fallen** every year.

23. Two cats **fought** last night.

24. They have **fought** every night this week.

25. A bird **flew** by.

26. The bird has **flown** to its nest.

More Practice Lesson 75

Complete this irregular verb chart by writing the past and past participle forms of each verb.

VERB	PAST	PAST PARTICIPLE
1. get	got	(has) gotten
2. give	gave	(has) given
3. go	went	(has) gone
4. hang (execute)	hanged	(has) hanged
5. hang (suspend)	hung	(has) hung
6. hide	hid	(has) hidden or hid
7. hold	held	(has) held
8. keep	kept	(has) kept
9. lay (place)	laid	(has) laid
10. lead	led	(has) led
11. lend	lent	(has) lent
12. lie (recline)	lay	(has) lain
13. lie (deceive)	lied	(has) lied
14. lose	lost	(has) lost
15. make	made	(has) made
16. mistake	mistook	(has) mistaken
17. put	put	(has) put
18. ride	rode	(has) ridden
19. rise	rose	(has) risen
20. run	ran	(has) run
21. see	saw	(has) seen
22. sell	sold	(has) sold

**More Practice
Lesson 75
(Continued)**

Choose the correct verb form for each sentence.

1. Bob **gave** a report to the committee.

2. He has **given** a report each month.

3. Joshua **went** to a new country.

4. He has **gone** alone.

5. I **hung** a picture on the wall.

6. I have **hung** three pictures.

7. The pirate **hid** the treasure.

8. He **held** a gold coin.

9. He has **kept** the coin for years.

10. Jan **laid** the book on the table.

11. She has **laid** several books on the table.

12. He was tired, so he **lay** on the bed.

13. He has **lain** there for hours!

14. Christie **lost** her keys again.

15. She has **lost** them twice already today.

16. I **made** a mistake.

17. I have **made** many mistakes.

18. Yesterday, I **put** toothpaste on my hairbrush.

19. I have never before **put** toothpaste on anything but a toothbrush.

20. The sun **rose** at 6 a.m.

21. It has **risen** earlier each morning.

22. I **saw** you earlier.

23. I have **seen** you every day.

24. He **sold** his bike.

25. He has **sold** two bikes.

Complete this irregular verb chart by writing the past and past participle forms of each verb.

	VERB	PAST	PAST PARTICIPLE
1.	set	set	(has) set
2.	shake	shook	(has) shaken
3.	shine (light)	shone	(has) shone
4.	shine (polish)	shined	(has) shined
5.	shut	shut	(has) shut
6.	sit	sat	(has) sat
7.	slay	slew	(has) slain
8.	sleep	slept	(has) slept
9.	spring	sprang, sprung	(has) sprung
10.	stand	stood	(has) stood
11.	strive	strove	(has) striven
12.	swim	swam	(has) swum
13.	swing	swung	(has) swung
14.	take	took	(has) taken
15.	teach	taught	(has) taught
16.	tell	told	(has) told
17.	think	thought	(has) thought
18.	wake	woke	(has) woken
19.	weave	wove	(has) woven
20.	wring	wrung	(has) wrung
21.	write	wrote	(has) written

Choose the correct verb form for each sentence.

1. Jen **set** the table.

2. She has **set** it for each meal.

3. She **shook** his hand.

4. She has **shaken** many hands.

5. A light **shone** in the darkness.

6. The light has **shone** each night.

7. Rich **shined** his shoes.

8. He has **shined** several pairs of shoes today.

9. Isabel **shut** the library door.

10. She has **shut** the door every evening.

11. She **sat** on a rock.

12. She has **sat** there for hours.

13. I **slept** twelve hours last night.

14. I have never **slept** so long.

15. He **stood** on his feet.

16. He has **stood** there all day.

17. I **swam** a mile this morning.

18. I have **swum** three miles this week.

19. He **took** his dog to the vet.

20. He has **taken** Spot to the vet twice this month.

21. Alba and Blanca **taught** me to speak Spanish.

22. They have **taught** me many new words.

23. Ilbea **told** me a secret.

24. Has she **told** you the news?

25. I **thought** you were wise.

26. I have always **thought** that.

Underline each adverb in these sentences.

1. Today, I was <u>somewhat</u> surprised when a peacock strutted <u>proudly</u> into my yard.

2. When he <u>carelessly</u> stepped on our flowers, I was <u>rather</u> annoyed.

3. I was <u>completely</u> amazed at the dazzling colors in his tail feathers.

4. I had <u>never</u> seen anything like it <u>before</u>.

5. I <u>quickly</u> grabbed my camera to photograph this lovely sight.

6. <u>Then</u>, with a thump, a peahen landed <u>clumsily</u> on my roof.

7. I'm <u>not quite</u> sure why they came <u>here</u>.

8. The peacock <u>hungrily</u> gobbled the petunias that we had <u>so</u> <u>carefully</u> planted.

9. The peahen <u>eagerly</u> uprooted some daffodils and <u>gingerly</u> nibbled the ferns that waved <u>too</u> <u>close</u> to her beak.

10. Screeching <u>loudly</u>, the two birds <u>soon</u> flew <u>away</u>.

11. I <u>really</u> hope Mom won't be <u>too</u> upset when she sees the <u>extremely</u> messy condition of the garden.

12. I'm <u>so</u> glad the peafowl visited <u>here</u>!

13. I hope they come <u>back</u> <u>tomorrow</u>.

14. I could <u>simply</u> invite them <u>inside</u>.

15. If they'd sit <u>down</u> <u>politely</u>, I would <u>happily</u> offer them some broccoli and carrots.

16. I can <u>almost</u> see them <u>now</u>.

17. Would they <u>gracefully</u> accept my hospitality?

18. Would Mom <u>ever</u> forgive me?

Replace commas with semicolons where they are needed in these sentences.

1. Cities with Native American names include Wichita, Kansas; Tucson, Arizona; Tallahassee, Florida; Minneapolis, Minnesota; and Seminole, Oklahoma.

2. The sales representative passes through Denver, Colorado; Austin, Texas; and Memphis, Tennessee.

3. Damien plays drums; Annie plays the saxophone, the flute, and the trumpet.

4. Broccoli, okra, and asparagus are vegetables; tangerines, apricots, and nectarines are fruits.

5. Dr. Hagelganz spoke this week; moreover, Foster Shannon will speak next week.

6. James washed the car, cleaned the house, and mowed the lawn; consequently, he fell asleep during the movie.

7. I like to bake cookies, cakes, and pies; however, I've never made an eclair.

8. In November a pound of bananas cost 29¢; in December, 39¢; in January, 49¢; in February, 59¢; and in March, 69¢.

9. I worked all day; therefore, I finished the project on time.

10. Donald and Tim will be there; also, Cecilia will come if she can.

11. She enjoys planting trees; for example, she planted two oaks and a cedar last fall.

12. Joe cleaned the kitchen; furthermore, he organized all the cupboards and drawers.

13. The weather was cold; nevertheless, Bob hiked to the top of the mountain.

14. He wore new shoes; as a result, he has blisters on his feet.

15. Would you rather visit Paris, France; Rome, Italy; Juneau, Alaska; or Moscow, Russia?

Silly Story #5

(After Lesson 93)

Instructions to Teacher Have the student number a blank, lined piece of paper from 1 to 26. Ask him or her to write an example of the indicated part of speech beside each number. Proceed slowly, and frequently question the student to be sure he or she has written a correct example of the part of speech you have requested for each blank space in the story.

After the list has been completed, give the student a copy of "Packing a Suitcase." Ask him or her to write each word from the list in the blank space with the corresponding number. Then ask the student to read the story aloud.

Packing a Suitcase Three friends, (1) _proper noun, person_ , (2) _proper noun, person_ , and (3) _proper noun, person_ , were planning a long trip to (4) _proper noun, place_ . (5) _adverb that tells "how"_, they began thinking about what they should pack for this (6) _descriptive adjective_ journey.

First, they found the (7) _superlative adjective_ suitcases. Then they looked (8) _adverb that tells "where"_ and (9) _adverb that tells "where"_ for some stylish (10) _descriptive adjective_ clothes. (11) _adverb that tells "when"_ they (12) _past tense action verb_ as they packed (13) _concrete plural noun_ and (14) _concrete plural noun_ in case of bad weather.

Full of anticipation and (15) _abstract noun_ , the friends (16) _adverb that tells "how"_ loaded their suitcases with

(17) <u>number adjective</u> (18) <u>concrete plural noun</u> . They wondered

if they should also bring some (19) <u>concrete plural noun</u> .

They borrowed (20) <u>proper noun (person), possessive case</u> earplugs and

(21) <u>proper noun (person), possessive case</u> toothbrush for the trip, and they

(22) <u>adverb that tells "how"</u> purchased a (23) <u>concrete singular noun</u> . As

they packed, they discussed (24) <u>abstract noun</u> and

(25) <u>abstract noun</u> until late at night.

Unfortunately, the three friends were too exhausted to

travel the next day. "Forget the trip," they said. "Let's

(26) <u>action verb: first person plural, present tense, intransitive</u> instead."

More Practice Lesson 98

Insert apostrophes where they are needed in these sentences.

1. He couldn't remember whether he'd last seen the doctor back in '47 or '52.

2. Don't you want to remove the extra *x*'s from this page?

3. In her letters, Grandma writes *x*'s and *o*'s to indicate kisses and hugs.

4. Mrs. Jones yelled, "Good mornin'!" to her neighbor.

5. "Oh my," exclaimed Sue, "Those ladies were just walkin' and talkin', and they never saw the thief comin'!"

6. Can't you see that I haven't time to go out for lunch?

7. She graduated from high school with the class of '70, but I graduated in '66.

8. Isn't her integrity obvious?

9. We're going to class. Aren't you?

10. They're going to class also.

11. Wouldn't you like to join us?

12. Shouldn't we try to be punctual?

13. She'll come if she can.

14. We'll forgive her if she doesn't come.

15. I've written him, but he hasn't responded.

16. She'd received nothing but *A*'s all year.

17. They couldn't see through the fog.

18. They weren't sure where their cars were.

19. He doesn't know you're home.

20. She hasn't called yet, but she'll call before noon.

For 1–4, write whether the sentence is declarative, interrogative, exclamatory, or imperative.

1. A punctual worker clocks in on time. _____
(1)

2. Do you think pushing to the front of the line is being considerate? _____
(1)

3. Stay in line. _____
(1)

4. Look out! _____
(1)

For sentences 5–7, circle the simple subject and underline the simple predicate.

5. Did you understand the moral of the story?
(2)

6. He found the simple subject of the sentence.
(2)

7. Oliver Twist worked in a workhouse.
(2)

For 8–15, circle the best word to complete each sentence.

8. I trust that Moe will complete the task because he is (humorous, reliable, funny).
(3)

9. Good students do not (waste, waist) time.
(5)

10. *Weight* and *wait* are (homophones, homonyms, antonyms).
(4)

11. (*Moral, Respectful, Punctual*) means "on time."
(1)

12. A (considerate, considerable, suspicious) person is thoughtful of others.
(1)

13. A moral person is concerned with right and (left, wrong, grades).
(2)

14. *Respectful* means "courteous" and "(punctual, smart, polite)."
(3)

15. The prefix *homo-* means "(same, opposite, irritable)."
(4)

For 16–18, write whether the word group is a sentence fragment, run-on sentence, or complete sentence.

16. The athlete ran his fastest mile ever. _____
(3)

17. Tossing his yo-yo to the ground. _____
(3)

18. A complete sentence has both a subject and a predicate. _____
(2)

Make complete sentences from fragments 19 and 20. Answers will vary.

19. Tumbled down the hill. _____
(3, 4)

20. After combing his hair. _____
(3, 4)

For 21 and 22, add periods and capital letters to correct the run-on sentences.

21. Jill needs to go to the grocery store she also needs to take clothes to the cleaners.
(3, 4)

22. The tourist desires to see the Forum he also wants to see the Coliseum while visiting Los
(3, 4) Angeles.

For sentences 23 and 24, circle the action verb.

23. The volcano erupted furiously.
(5)

24. Hot, glowing lava flowed down the mountain.
(5)

25. Replace the underlined verb with one that is more descriptive: _____
(5)

The horse <u>went</u> down the hill.

For 1 and 2, write whether the noun is singular or plural.

1. nails _____
(10)

2. hammer _____
(10)

For 3–6, write whether the noun is feminine, masculine, indefinite, or neuter.

3. manatee _____
(10)

4. bull _____
(10)

5. hen _____
(10)

6. cage _____
(10)

7. Circle the compound noun from this list: horseshoe, licorice, sugar
(10)

8. Circle the possessive noun from this sentence: A Siamese cat's eyes appear slanted.
(10)

9. From memory, write 23 common helping verbs. _____
(9)

_____

_____

_____

10. Circle the simple subject of this sentence: Rain continued to pour from the threatening skies.
(2)

11. Underline the simple predicate of this sentence, and circle the helping verb:
(2, 9)

The postman will bring the package to the door.

For 12–14, write whether the word group is a complete sentence, sentence fragment, or run-on sentence.

12. The sun peeked through the clouds then the rainbow appeared. _____
(3)

13. With the crispness of the air in the early morning hours before dawn. _____
(3)

14. Flaunting its full range of colors, the rainbow paralyzed its admirers. _____
(3)

15. Circle each abstract noun from this list: thought, memory, lemon
(8)

16. Circle each collective noun from this list: jury, pillow, committee
(8)

17. Unscramble these words to make an interrogative sentence.
_(1)_

        rainbow   you   seen   have   ever   a   brilliant

_____

For 18–25, circle the best word to complete each sentence.

18. Sun bathers (lie, lay) in the sun.
_(10)_

19. A (respectful, willpower) citizen takes down the American flag at dusk.
_(3)_

20. The hair of a hog is (coarse, course) rather than fine.
_(8)_

21. Please (lie, lay) my photo album on this table when you're finished looking at it.
_(10)_

22. Weston wore a belt around his (waist, waste).
_(5)_

23. Let's not (waist, waste) water by taking long showers.
_(5)_

24. When Kristina found a diamond necklace in the library, she took it to the "lost and found," for
_(6)_ she has (geography, integrity, kleptomania).

25. Caleb will learn about rocks and minerals in his (biology, psychology, geology) class.
_(7)_

Give after Lesson 20.

1. For a–d, circle the correct verb form.
(15)

    (a) You (am, are, is)   (b) They (am, are, is)   (c) It (do, does)   (d) I (do, does)

For 2–7, write the plural of each noun.

2. penny _____
(13, 14)

3. mouse _____
(13, 14)

4. hiss _____
(10, 13)

5. radio _____
(13, 14)

6. cupful _____
(13, 14)

7. book _____
(10, 13)

8. Circle each letter that should be capitalized in the following:
(6, 12)

       william shakespeare wrote these lines of poetry:

          oh, my offense is rank, it smells to heaven.

          it hath the primal eldest curse upon 't . . .

9. Circle each helping verb in this sentence:
(9)

       I would have come sooner if you had called me.

For 10 and 11, circle the correct verb form to complete each sentence.

10. I (shall, will) drive to the airport.
(11)

11. The coach (toss, tosses) baseballs.
(7)

12. For a–d, write whether the noun is masculine, feminine, indefinite, neuter, or abstract.
(10)

    (a) truck _____   (b) holiday _____

    (c) grandmother _____   (d) uncle _____

13. Circle each possessive noun in this list: children's, boys, boy's, teachers, teachers', ladies, lady's
(8, 10)

For 14–16, write whether the word group is a sentence fragment, run-on sentence, or complete sentence.

14. The squid's long, soft body with a large head and two huge eyes. _____
(3)

15. The squid has an ink sac it helps the squid make a quick, undercover escape. _____
(3)

16. A squid's eyes have characteristics similar to a human's. _____
(3)

17. Write whether the sentence below is declarative, imperative, interrogative, or exclamatory.
(1)

The squid is a carnivorous mollusk. _____

18. Circle the subject and underline the verb phrase (simple predicate) in sentences a and b.
(2)

(a) The giant squid can grow up to sixty feet long.

(b) It might weigh more than 1000 pounds.

Circle the correct word to complete sentences 19–25.

19. She rode a three-wheeled (bicycle, tricycle, unicycle).
(13)

20. The prefix *bio-* means "(earth, life, under)."
(11)

21. That shaggy dog keeps scratching (it's, its) ears.
(15)

22. (It's, Its) never too late to say you're sorry.
(15)

23. The prefix (*uni-, bio-, sub-*) means "under."
(14)

24. A unicycle has (one, two, three) wheel(s).
(13)

25. Ryan worked each math problem very carefully, for he is (punctual, bilingual, conscientious).
(12)

Give after Lesson 25.

1. Circle each letter that should be capitalized in a and b.
(6, 20)

    (a) the book was titled <u>the people of pineapple place</u>.

    (b) patrick henry cried, "give me liberty, or give me death."

2. Write whether the underlined perfect tense verb phrase is past, present, or future perfect in
(19) sentences a–d.

    (a) The girls <u>will have shopped</u> for six hours. _____ perfect

    (b) Alisa <u>had failed</u> to check her phone messages. _____ perfect

    (c) Elise and Oscar <u>have studied</u> for today's test. _____ perfect

    (d) Jordan <u>has memorized</u> the helping verbs. _____ perfect

3. Circle the four prepositions from this list of words:
(17, 18)

lie	tricycle	persevere	to
with	walk	run	about
jump	skip	for	not

4. Circle the present participle of the verb *jump*:   (has) jumped   (is) jumping   jumped
(16)

5. Circle the four helping verbs from this list: moral, over, clown, have, red, suit, should, hop, shall,
(9) may, loyalty

For 6–11, circle the correct verb form.

6. I (am, are, is)
(15)

7. I (have, has)
(15)

8. They (does, do)
(15)

9. We (shall, will)
(11)

10. Julian (shop, shops)
(7)

11. Julian and I (play, plays)
(7)

For 12–14, write the plural form of each noun.

12. mouse _____
(13, 14)

13. deer _____
(13, 14)

14. woman _____
(13, 14)

15. For a–d, write whether the noun is masculine, feminine, indefinite, neuter, or abstract.
(8, 10)

(a) grandparent _____   (b) love _____

(c) father _____   (d) daughter _____

16. For a–d, write whether the word group is a sentence fragment, run-on sentence, or complete
(3) sentence.

(a) The manatee is a gentle creature it spends its day resting, migrating, and grazing.
_____

(b) The manatee is an endangered species. _____

(c) The West African, Amazonian, and West Indian species. _____

(d) I've never seen a manatee have you? _____

17. Write whether the sentence below is declarative, imperative, exclamatory, or interrogative.
(1)

Is the dugong a relative of the manatee? _____

18. Circle the simple subject and underline the verb in this sentence:
(2)

The dugong live in areas around Australia.

Circle the correct word to complete sentences 19–25.

19. (Who's, Whose) painting is this?
(19)

20. (It's, Its) Mary Cassatt's painting.
(15)

21. A prodigious nose is (broken, red, large).
(20)

22. I don't know (who's, whose) canary that is.
(19)

23. (Who's, Whose) helping Karlo in the kitchen?
(19)

24. Taylor has (to, too, two) much homework.
(18)

25. Remy flew (to, too, two) Hawaii last weekend.
(18)

Give after Lesson 30.

Circle the correct word to complete sentences 1–11.

1. The famous actor Jimmy Durante had a (reliable, prodigious) nose.
(20)

2. April has (fewer, less) days than May.
(21)

3. A (linking, helping, action) verb "links" the subject of a sentence to the rest of the predicate.
(22)

4. The sentence below is (declarative, interrogative, imperative, exclamatory):
(1)

That cat scratched me!

5. The following is a (sentence fragment, run-on sentence, complete sentence):
(3)

The cat's scratch bled.

6. This proper noun is (abstract, concrete): Amazon River
(8)

7. A monologue is performed by (one, two, many) actor(s).
(25)

8. Morgan read the (whole, hole) book in one day.
(24)

9. A mouse chewed a (whole, hole) in Helen's backpack.
(24)

10. The team felt they would win; their (moral, morale) was high.
(23)

11. Sara is kind and caring; she has (perseverance, compassion, disdain) for the less fortunate.
(22)

12. Write the plural form of a–d:
(13, 14)

(a) penny _____ (b) trout _____ (c) man _____ (d) child _____

Circle each letter that should be capitalized in 13–15.

13. julius caesar commented, "but, for my own part, it was greek to me."
(6, 20)

14. william shakespeare wrote *julius caesar*.
(6, 20)

15. i saw *julius caesar* performed at the charleston square theatre.
(6, 20)

16. Circle each preposition that you find in this sentence:
(17, 18)

The man in the clown costume came with me to the circus.

17. Circle the four helping verbs in this list: upon, wheel, be, hammer, cart, shall, have, bag, sock, must
(9)

18. For a–d, circle the correct irregular verb form.
(15)

    (a) She (am, is, are)   (b) They (do, does)   (c) You (has, have)   (d) He (do, does)

19. Circle the present perfect verb phrase in this sentence: Erin has completed the marathon.
(19)

20. Circle the future perfect verb phrase in this sentence: Soon, Kim will have finished her sixth
(19) race.

21. Circle the future progressive verb phrase in this sentence: Ruth and Mitzi will be celebrating
(21) their fifteenth birthdays on Saturday.

22. Circle the future perfect progressive verb phrase in this sentence: This September, we shall have
(21) been living in Monrovia for 14 years.

Diagram the simple subject, simple predicate, and direct object of sentences 23 and 24.

23. The boy patted the dog.
(23, 25)

24. The dog licked the boy.
(23, 25)

25. For a and b, circle to indicate whether each word group is a phrase or a clause.
(24)

    (a) swallowed the cold milk   phrase   clause

    (b) after the fish swam away   phrase   clause

Give after Lesson 35.

Circle the correct word(s) to complete sentences 1–12.

1. Have you ever visited the (Capitol, Capital) Building in Washington, D.C.?
(30)

2. The athlete's (faint, feint) of injury did not fool all the spectators.
(28)

3. The (progressive, perfect) verb tense shows action that has been completed.
(19, 21)

4. (Articles, Pronouns) are the most commonly used adjectives, and they are also the shortest—*a,*
(28) *an, the.*

5. *His, her, their, your, its, our,* and *my* are examples of (possessive, descriptive) adjectives.
(27, 28)

6. The sentence below is (declarative, imperative, interrogative, exclamatory):
(1)

There's a shark in these waters!

7. The word group below is a (sentence fragment, run-on sentence, complete sentence):
(3)

Born with a knack for invention.

8. An incredible story is (very, not, almost) believable.
(29)

9. My (monopoly, capital, conscience) makes me aware of right and wrong.
(26)

10. A thunderstorm might (affect, effect) our outdoor activities.
(27)

11. Will the storm have an (affect, effect) on your activities?
(27)

12. The hungry bear opened (it's, its) mouth and growled.
(15)

13. Circle the abstract noun from this list: punchball, blacktop, chalkboard, knowledge, hallway
(8)

14. Circle each possessive noun in this list: wives, wife's, sons', sons, aunt's, aunts, collies, collie's
(10)

15. Write the plural form of the singular noun *knife.* _____
(13, 14)

For 16 and 17, circle each letter that should be capitalized.

16. hamlet cries, "frailty, thy name is woman."
(6, 20)

17. dear mr. carruthers,
(6, 29)

we leave tomorrow for new england. i can't wait to taste the chowder.

sincerely, miss renner

18. Circle each preposition in this sentence: Haley, the energetic toddler with red hair, slid down the
(17, 18) slide and sat on the swings in the shade.

19. Circle the four helping verbs from this list: what, whom, been, did, globe, where, should, shall
(9)

20. Circle the linking verb in this sentence: Another name for bananas is "hands with little fingers."
(22)

21. For a–d, circle the correct irregular verb form.
(15)

    (a) I (am, is, are)   (b) He (do, does)   (c) They (has, have)   (d) She (has, have)

22. Circle the present progressive verb phrase in this sentence: This delicious banana is providing
(21) me with vitamin C and potassium.

23. For sentences a and b, write whether the verb is an action or linking verb.
(5, 22)

    (a) The captain <u>felt</u> seasick. _____   (b) She <u>felt</u> the boat rock. _____

24. Circle each adjective in this sentence: The brown velvety rabbit sported long, slender ears and a
(27, 28) moist black nose.

25. Fill in the diagram to the right using each word
(25, 28) of this sentence: Enthusiastic skiers appreciate
steep, beautiful mountains.

Give after Lesson 40.

Circle the correct word to complete sentences 1–11.

1. The prefix that means "through," "across," "between," or "apart" is (*mono-, homo-, dia-, bi-*).
(35)

2. The waiter will (pore, pour, poor) milk into the glasses.
(34)

3. This sentence is (declarative, imperative, interrogative, exclamatory): Drink that glass of milk
(1) now.

4. The word group below is a (sentence fragment, run-on sentence, complete sentence).
(3)

When wood burns, energy changes to heat and light no energy is lost.

5. This word group is a (phrase, clause): because they have no legs
(24)

6. The noun or pronoun that follows a preposition is called the (subject, object, modifier) of the
(33) preposition.

7. The diameter is the distance (around, across, outside) a circle.
(35)

8. The prefix (*dia-, bio-, post-*) means "after."
(32)

9. A proper noun begins with a (capitol, capital) letter.
(30)

10. While rowing upstream, Daniel lost an (oar, ore, or).
(33)

11. *Postmortem* means "(after, before, through) death."
(32)

12. Circle the concrete noun from this list: Portuguese, language, Thanksgiving, wood, legalism
(8)

13. Circle the feminine noun from this list: grandmother, brother, physician, pen, shoe
(10)

14. Write the plural of the noun *sky*. _____
(13)

15. Circle each letter that should be capitalized in this humorous rhyme about chemical formulas:
(6, 12)

johnny had a stomachache.
he hasn't anymore.
for what he thought was H_2O
was H_2SO_4.

16. Circle the four prepositions in this sentence:
(17, 18)

One of the fundamental laws in physics and chemistry is called the law of the conservation of
energy.

Underline the prepositional phrase and circle the object of the preposition in sentences 17 and 18.

17. The instructor laid the test on the desk.
(17, 33)

18. The snake in the fourth display is poisonous.
(17, 33)

19. Circle the word from this list that is *not* a helping verb: is, am, are, was, were, why, be, being,
(9) been, has, had, have, do, does, did, shall, will, should, would, can, could, may, might, must

20. Circle the linking verb in this sentence: Most snakes are harmless.
(22)

21. For a–d, circle the correct irregular verb form.
(15)

    (a) we (was, were)   (b) it (do, does)   (c) you (has, have)   (d) he (do, does)

For sentences 22 and 23, underline the verb and circle the direct object if there is one. Then circle
"transitive" or "intransitive." (Hint: A transitive verb has a direct object.)

22. Snakes can slither along the ground at up to six miles per hour. (transitive, intransitive)
(25, 32)

23. Reptiles use the sun to keep warm. (transitive, intransitive)
(25, 32)

24. Circle the indirect object in this sentence: Mrs. Smith gave the children some cookies.
(35)

25. Fill in the diagram to the right using each word
(25, 35) of this sentence: Debby's hot salsa gave her
brother a pain in his stomach.

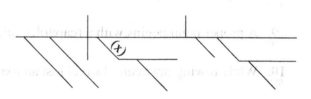

Circle the correct word to complete sentences 1–12.

1. The students chose their future occupations with (prudence, perseverance, compassion).
(36)

2. Can you (so, sow, sew) my ripped seam?
(37)

3. This sentence is (declarative, imperative, interrogative, exclamatory): Have you ever seen a gopher snake?
(1)

4. This word group is a (sentence fragment, run-on sentence, complete sentence): Snakes sense vibrations they sense them with the lower jaw.
(3)

5. (Commas, Periods, Quotation marks) help the reader to know where a sentence begins and ends.
(36)

6. (Coordinating conjunctions, Verbs, Nouns) join parts of a sentence that are equal.
(37)

7. (Nouns, Adjectives, Correlative conjunctions) always come in pairs.
(39)

8. Peter chooses his friends carefully, or with (injustice, perseverance, discretion).
(36)

9. Maria and Alexandra met (there, they're, their) friend Heather at the library.
(38)

10. Please (accept, except) my apology.
(40)

11. Martin is tired, but he keeps working, for he has (independence, injustice, perseverance).
(16)

12. Nathan and Chase are talking to one another. They are having a (dialogue, diagonal, monopoly).
(35)

13. Write the plural of *piano*. _____
(14)

14. Write the correct verb form: Jarad _____ (present tense of *empty*) the trash.
(7)

15. Circle each letter that should be capitalized in this sentence: the teacher required each student to read *the adventures of huckleberry finn*.
(20)

16. Circle the two prepositions from this sentence: Like other reptiles, snakes have a backbone of small bones called vertebrae.
(17)

17. Circle the word from this list that is *not* a helping verb: is, am, are, was, were, be, being, been, while, has, have, had, may, might, must, can, could, do, does, did, shall, will, should, would
(9)

18. Circle each coordinating conjunction from this list: and, but, yet, seem, or, after, not, for, so
(37)

19. Circle the correlative conjunctions in this sentence: Not only Maria but also Angela attended the
(39) concert in the park.

20. Underline the prepositional phrase and circle the object of the preposition in this sentence:
(17, 33)

What is the national symbol of the United States?

21. Circle the entire verb phrase in this sentence: The football coach has chalked the field.
(9, 19)

22. Circle each linking verb in this list: look, scratch, feel, taste, smell, write, sound, seem, appear,
(22) cook, grow, become, remain, run, stay

23. Add periods where they are needed in this sentence: The Rev R U Glad delivered a humorous
(36) monologue at the park on St James St at 9 a m on Sunday

Complete the diagrams of sentences 24 and 25.

24. The flower girl gave the wedding guests rose
(25, 35) petals from her basket.

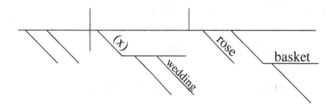

25. Tigers and leopards not only fascinate but also
(38, 39) frighten explorers.

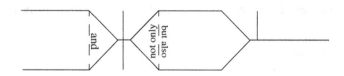

Give after Lesson 50.

Circle the correct word to complete sentences 1–10.

1. The prefix *ultra-* means "(not, extreme, after)."
(44)

2. The prefix *mal-* means "(one, life, bad)."
(41)

3. This word group is a (sentence fragment, run-on sentence, complete sentence): A belt around his
(3) waist.

4. She (have, has) two cats.
(15)

5. Positive, comparative, and superlative adjectives are known as (comparison, descriptive)
(27, 45) adjectives.

6. The school (principle, principal) called a meeting of all the teachers.
(43)

7. Evelyn will (sit, set) her grammar book on your desk.
(42)

8. Stephen would like to (sit, set) beside Johnny because (there, they're, their) friends.
(42)

9. Kelly appreciates Veronica's (advise, advice).
(45)

10. Timothy will (so, sew, sow) the carrot seeds and then cover them with soil.
(37)

11. Circle the collective noun from this list: philosophy, classroom, United Nations, thumb, Mrs.
(8) Gonzáles

Circle each letter that should be capitalized in 12 and 13.

12. the long novel *gone with the wind* tells about life in the south during the civil war in america.
(26, 29)

13. dear aunt frances,
(26, 29)
          I have learned four different ways to cook okra during my visit to the south.

                    love,

                    jaime

14. The plural of the noun *prefix* is _____.
(13)

15. Underline the prepositional phrase and circle the object of the preposition in this sentence:
(17, 33)

          Mother's Day is a special day of the year.

16. Circle the verb phrase in this sentence: Our class will be going to the museum on Thursday.
(9, 21)

17. For sentences a and b, write whether the underlined verb is action or linking.
(5, 22)

    (a) The music <u>sounded</u> harmonious. _____

    (b) The children <u>sounded</u> the bell when the Mother's Day breakfast was ready. _____

18. Circle the two possessive adjectives in this sentence: After Anna Jarvis's mother passed away in
(28) 1907, Anna convinced her mother's church to set aside the second Sunday of May to honor all
mothers.

19. Circle the correlative conjunctions in this sentence: Not only the church of Anna Jarvis's
(39) mother, but also churches across the United States began to celebrate Mother's Day.

20. Circle the predicate nominative in this sentence: Flowers are the most common gift on Mother's
(41) Day.

For 21–23, write whether the italicized word is nominative case, objective case, or possessive case.

21. Denmark, Finland, and Turkey, are other *countries* that celebrate Mother's Day.
(42, 43) _____

22. Actually, the tradition of honoring mothers dates back to ancient *Greece*. _____
(12, 43)

23. In 1914, *President Woodrow Wilson* declared Mother's Day an official holiday.
(42, 43) _____

Complete the diagrams of sentences 24 and 25.

24. Fido tasted the frosting on the cake.
(25)

25. Mother's Day became important and meaningful.
(44, 38)

Test 10

Give after Lesson 55.

Circle the correct word to complete sentences 1–13.

1. The electric company will (advice, advise) consumers of an upcoming blackout.
(45)

2. (Malnutrition, Maltreatment, Maladjustment) is the result of a poor diet.
(41)

3. This word group is a (sentence fragment, run-on sentence, complete sentence): Have you ever
(3) fished for salmon?

4. The gender of the noun *assistant* is (masculine, feminine, indefinite, neuter).
(10)

5. The past participle of the verb *dance* is (*danced, dancing*).
(16)

6. Our electrical shortage is the (baddest, worst) one in several decades.
(45, 46)

7. Washington Avenue is (wide, wider, widest) than Lincoln Boulevard.
(45)

8. A fishing expert (do, does, done) catch many salmon.
(15)

9. Jazmyne, (may, can) I eat lunch with you today?
(48)

10. Jack found the missing puzzle (piece, peace) on the floor.
(49)

11. An ultraconservative person is (very, not, slightly) conservative.
(44)

12. Tomorrow morning, Jenna will (rays, raise, raze) the American flag again.
(46)

13. Did Jenna (break, brake) Norman's mechanical pencil?
(47)

Circle each letter that should be capitalized in 14 and 15.

14. have you read jack london's <u>the call of the wild</u>?
(6, 20)

15. the largest salmon is the pacific salmon.
(30, 31)

16. The plural of *salmon* is _____.
(14)

17. Circle the four words from this list that are *not* prepositions: alongside, concerning, species,
(17) regarding, underneath, parents, amid, below, spawned, excepting, from, conditions, opposite, like, since, to

18. Underline each prepositional phrase and circle the object of each preposition in this sentence: A
(17, 33) salmon can be classified by species, by the river of its birth, and by the season its parents spawned.

19. Circle the verb phrase in this sentence: Seven species of salmon were experiencing frightening
(21) decreases in population.

20. For sentences a and b, circle to show whether the underlined verb is transitive or intransitive.
(32)

(a) The man <u>swam</u> the English Channel. (transitive, intransitive)

(b) The man <u>swam</u> steadily. (transitive, intransitive)

21. Circle the sentence below that is written correctly.
(30)

I like that kind of a pie.   I like that kind of pie.

22. Add periods and commas as needed in this sentence: The baseball fans ate popcorn salted
(36, 47) peanuts hotdogs and frozen malts

23. Write whether the italicized word in this sentence is nominative, objective, or possessive
(42, 43) case: The shortstop caught a line *drive* during the seventh inning of the baseball game.
_____ case

24. Circle the appositive in this sentence: Babe Ruth, a famous baseball player, was inducted into
(48) the Hall of Fame many years ago.

25. Diagram this sentence in the space to the
(22, 44) right: That Boston fern looks thirsty.

Circle the correct word to complete sentences 1–9.

1. The pilot coasted his airplane into the (hanger, hangar).
(52)

2. The icemaker in our refrigerator breaks down (continually, continuously).
(54)

3. This fish is the (baddest, worst) I've ever eaten!
(46)

4. I (shall, will) study the Boer War in the near future.
(11)

5. (Can, May) Norman tighten the hand (break, brake) on his bicycle?
(48, 47)

6. The value of a vehicle might (substitute, depreciate, maltreat) as time goes on.
(53)

7. Austin and John (right, write, wright, rite) humorous essays.
(50)

8. Allison hung Hailey's coat on a (hanger, hangar).
(52)

9. Samuel, Dylan, and Kenneth have signed a (peace, piece) treaty.
(49)

10. Circle the four words in this list that are *not* prepositions: inside, into, like, near, of, off, on, onto,
(17) flutter, glide, opposite, out, marine, outside, over, past, aquarium, regarding, round

11. For sentences a and b, circle to show whether the underlined verb is transitive or intransitive.
(32)

    (a) The candle <u>glowed</u> faintly in the hallway. (transitive, intransitive)

    (b) The roaring fire <u>consumed</u> the logs. (transitive, intransitive)

12. Write the (a) past tense and (b) past participle of the irregular verb *drink*.
(16, 54)

    (a) _____   (b) _____

13. Add commas and periods as needed in this sentence:
(49)

    Dr Georgia L Banks Ph D the chairperson of Exotic Felines explained that there is
    actually no such cat as a panther

14. Circle the coordinating conjunction in this sentence: Lions, tigers, leopards, and jaguars belong
(37) to the genus *Panthera*.

15. Write whether the italicized nouns in this sentence are nominative, objective, or possessive case:
(42, 43)

    Leopards and *jaguars* have tan coats with black spots. _____ case

16. Circle the appositive in this sentence: Our school mascot, the black panther, is just a leopard in
(48) disguise.

17. Underline the pronoun and circle its antecedent in this sentence: Just because Max can't see the
(51) black spots on a black leopard doesn't mean they aren't there.

18. Circle each pronoun from this list that is third person plural: he, him, she, her, they, them, their,
(51) his, hers

19. Circle each nominative case pronoun in this list: me, him, I, she, them, they, he, her, we, us
(55)

Circle the nominative case pronoun in sentences 20 and 21.

20. The woman on the phone is (her, she).
(55)

21. (He, Him) and Sal play soccer.
(55)

22. Circle the sentence that is more polite (a or b).
(55)

    (a) The nominees were I and he.   (b) The nominees were he and I.

23. Circle each letter that should be capitalized in this sentence:
(6, 29)

    leopards can be found in africa, the middle east, and asia.

Diagram sentences 24 and 25 in the space to the right.

24. The zoo exhibits both leopards and jaguars.
(25, 38)

25. Leopards and jaguars are carnivorous animals.
(38, 41)

Give after Lesson 65.

Circle the correct words to complete sentences 1–14.

1. The committee believes that (your, you're) the best person for the job.
(56)

2. Josephine has two sisters and one brother, or three (siblings, hangars, pieces).
(59)

3. The following word group is a (phrase, clause): when one thinks of nationalism
(24)

4. Of the three countries, Italy was the (more, most) successful in her struggle for independence.
(46)

5. A predicate (nominative, subject, verb) follows a linking verb and renames the subject.
(41)

6. (Its, It's) leg appears to be fractured.
(15)

7. Esther and (her, she) walked to the shore.
(55)

8. Please go with José and (I, me) to deliver this meal.
(57)

9. The attendant gave Sergio and (him, he) the best seats in the stadium.
(57)

10. What time will the sun (raise, rise) tomorrow?
(58)

11. Ashley didn't have a pencil, so Patrick offered to (lend, borrow) her one.
(57)

12. Devin turned (right, write, wright, rite), not left, at the corner.
(50)

13. Please (leave, let) me go swimming!
(60)

14. Lauren will hang up (your, you're) coat for you.
(56)

15. Circle each letter that should be capitalized in this sentence: the gardenia bush smells most
(30, 31) fragrant in the spring.

16. Circle the entire verb phrase in this sentence: Italy had been united as a nation in 1861.
(9, 19)

17. Add periods as needed in this sentence: Please deliver this check for $1299 (twelve dollars and
(36, 40) ninety-nine cents) to our Lindsey St office

Add commas as needed to sentences 18 and 19.

18. No I cannot remember the last time we were in Seattle Washington.
(47, 56)

19. It rains all the time I seem to recall.
(56)

20. Unscramble these words to make a sentence with a personal pronoun as a predicate nominative:
(55)

mud   in   she   the   sow   was   the

_____

21. Circle each objective case personal pronoun from this list:
(57)

me   him   I   she   them   they   he   her   we   us

22. Write whether the italicized pronoun in this sentence is nominative, objective, or possessive case:
(58)

Yours is around the corner.   _____ case

Diagram sentences 23–25 in the space to the right.

23. Appaloosas   are   horses   with   distinct
(34, 41) markings.

24. Not only spots but also solid colors can
(38, 39) cover the Appaloosa.

25. The best riders are Jane and she.
(41, 59)

Circle the correct words to complete sentences 1–14.

1. A golfer yells "(for, fore, four)" to warn that a golf ball is coming.
(64)

2. The restaurant offered chocolate mousse and apple cobbler for (desert, dessert).
(63)

3. A (correlative, subordinating, coordinating) conjunction introduces a dependent clause.
(61)

4. Did you score (gooder, better, best) than your opponent in the speech contest?
(46)

5. Tedmond (knowed, knew, known) every answer on the test.
(54)

6. The woman with the umbrella is (her, she).
(55)

7. The person hiding in the garden was (me, I).
(55)

8. RuthAnn's chili was superb, while (ours, our's) was just so-so.
(58)

9. They spun the wool (theirselves, themselves).
(62)

10. The prefix (*frac-*, *geo-*, *poly-*) means "many."
(61)

11. Please (teach, learn) me how to speak Russian.
(62)

12. Aaron photographs reptiles in the (desert, dessert).
(63)

13. A polygon has (long, curved, many) sides.
(61)

14. Everyone (accept, except) Adrian had the wrong answer.
(40)

15. Circle the subordinating conjunction in this sentence:
(61)

I will persevere in my Spanish class until I have mastered the language.

16. Circle the verb in this sentence, and circle to show whether it is an action or linking verb:
(5, 22)

In the 1860s, the king of Prussia appointed a new prime minister. (action, linking)

17. In the blanks below, write the four principal parts of the verb *snip*.
(16)

    (a) present tense:_____   (b) present participle:_____

    (c) past tense:_____   (d) past participle:_____

18. Circle each adjective in this sentence: Prussia was a large, powerful state in Germany.
(27, 28)

19. Write whether the italicized noun in this sentence is in the nominative, objective, or possessive
(42, 43) case:

Otto von Bismarck, a nationalist, was the new *prime minister*. _____ case

20. Add commas as needed in this sentence:
(65)

"Unfortunately" explained Mrs. Schmidt "Bismarck was a ruthless leader."

21. Circle the appositive in this sentence: The Prussian king, Wilhelm I, was declared Kaiser of the
(48) united German states.

22. Circle the antecedent for the italicized pronoun in this sentence:
(51)

Bismarck was forced from office because *he* and Wilhelm's successor did not get along.

23. Circle the sentence that is more polite (a or b).
(57)

(a) The lemon meringue pie was for him and me.

(b) The lemon meringue pie was for me and him.

Diagram sentences 24 and 25 in the space to the right.

24. Yours is the best entry at the fair.
(34, 41)

25. Most people supported the new railroad, but
(64, 65) some people disliked the noise, dirt, and
danger.

Give after Lesson 75.

Circle the correct word to complete sentences 1–12.

1. The (arrogance, prudence, humility) of the university student offended many people.
(70)

2. José could not decide whether to attend summer school or to work a summer job. He had a
(66) (desertion, dilemma, peace).

3. A (verb, adjective, pronoun) takes the place of a noun.
(51)

4. The grateful recipient of a scholarship thanked (her, she) and them many times.
(57)

5. The sixth grader (which, who) wore size twelve shoes ran the fastest mile.
(66)

6. It was (me, I).
(55)

7. They (was, were) organized.
(15)

8. Did you (here, hear) Giancarlo's good news?
(68)

9. (Can, May) I borrow your pen?
(48)

10. The prefix (*frac-*, *hemi-*, *anti-*) means "against."
(65)

11. A polychromatic rug has (artificial, shiny, many) colors.
(61)

12. To prevent infection, Ayanna sprayed (hemistich, antiseptic, postscript) on Helen's wound.
(65)

13. Circle the entire verb phrase in this sentence:
(9, 21)

> We might have been discussing the effects of a violent tornado.

14. Circle the indirect object in this sentence: The chef broiled me a swordfish steak.
(35)

15. Circle each letter that should be capitalized in this sentence:
(29, 31)

> in the autumn, we see brilliant yellows, oranges, and reds on foliage in the east.

16. Circle the possessive adjective in this sentence: A strong tornado may leave its mark on the
(28, 60) landscape.

17. Circle the overused adjective in this sentence: It's neat that a tornado can drive a straw into a
(50) plank of wood.

18. Underline the dependent clause and circle the subordinating conjunction in this sentence:
(61)

> Unless it snows, I'll hike Mount Whitney tomorrow.

19. Add commas as needed to this sentence: On Friday February 6 2003 Grandma and Grandpa's
(47, 49) fiftieth wedding anniversary we sang their favorite song *When Irish Eyes Are Smiling*.

20. Unscramble these words to make a sentence with a personal pronoun as an object of a
(33, 53) preposition:

him   ate   surgeon   the   with   lunch

_____

Circle each reflexive or intensive pronoun in sentences 21 and 22.

21. We roofed the house ourselves.
(62)

22. A cat cleans itself by licking its fur.
(62)

23. Add quotation marks to this sentence: I may never see a blue whale, the marine biologist said.
(69, 70)

Diagram sentences 24 and 25 in the space to the right.

24. Have you memorized a portion of that poem?
(25, 34)

25. Do Hoover and he like pickle sandwiches with mustard?
(23, 38)

Give after Lesson 80.

Circle the correct words to complete sentences 1–16.

1. The (sympathy, reconciliation, punctuality) of the old enemies was long overdue.
(75)

2. The tiny terrier (beared, bared, devised) his teeth at the enormous Rottweiler.
(74)

3. The Archbishop of York has (flee, fled) to Canterbury.
(74)

4. Our laundry has (lied, lay, laid) in that same spot all morning.
(75)

5. Case indicates how (pronouns, italics, quotation marks) are used in a sentence.
(58)

6. That hilarious e-mail I received was from William and (she, her).
(57)

7. They baked, frosted, and decorated the wedding cake (theirselves, themselves).
(62)

8. Mr. Yu, (who, whom) you know, will visit tomorrow.   think: _you_ | know | ?
(66, 68)

9. Amelia (teared, tore, torn) up the silly note she wrote yesterday.
(54)

10. (Those, Them) oatmeal cookies are the best I have ever tasted.
(71)

11. Few (enjoy, enjoys) push-ups, sit-ups, and other physical exercises.
(72)

12. Using hotel (stationary, stationery), Kent wrote Jason a letter all about his vacation in Jackson
(73) Hole, Wyoming.

13. Natalie rescued Nicole from a large grizzly (bare, bear) in the forest.
(74)

14. Caleb, Mark, and Isaac had goosebumps, for they failed to (ware, wear, where) warm clothing.
(72)

15. Quadrupeds are animals having (for, fore, four) feet.
(64)

16. Miss Curtis's driver's license had expired; therefore, it was (fractious, invalid, semiprecious).
(55)

17. In the blanks below, write the four principal parts of the verb *shove*.
(16)

    (a) present tense:_____   (b) present participle:_____

    (c) past tense:_____   (d) past participle:_____

18. Circle each letter that should be capitalized:
(6, 26)

> my parents went to niagara falls on their honeymoon. part of niagara falls is in new york and part of it is in canada. mom and dad told me that on june 30, 1859, a frenchman named jean francois gravelet crossed the niagara river gorge on a tightrope.

19. Underline each prepositional phrase in this sentence, and circle the object of each preposition:
(17, 33)

> Whalebone is not bone, and it has none of the characteristics of bone.

20. Circle the verb in this sentence, and circle to show whether it is transitive or intransitive:
(32)

> Whalebone, or baleen, grows on the roof of the mouth in certain whales. (transitive, intransitive)

21. Add commas where necessary in this sentence:
(56, 63)

> According to some authorities the thin parallel plates of baleen can reach lengths of fifteen feet.

22. Circle each word that should be italicized in this sentence:
(73)

> The French say beau for handsome, but the Spanish say guapo.

23. Underline the dependent clause in this sentence, and circle the subordinating conjunction:
(61)

> I have more free time than she has.

Diagram sentences 24 and 25 in the space to the right.

24. The Archbishop of York is the Primate of England.
(23, 41)

25. Certain species of whales grow whalebone.
(25, 34)

Give after Lesson 85.

Circle the correct words to complete sentences 1–12.

1. The large number of holes in the yard (devised, implied, razed) the presence of gophers.
(79)

2. The (anxious, prodigious, conscientious) hikers watched dark storm clouds gather.
(78)

3. James Earle Fraser, an American sculptor, (make, made) the buffalo nickel with no particular
(75) Indian chief in mind.

4. (Whoever, Whomever) made this casserole is a good cook.
(66, 68)

5. The forest ranger gave (we, us) Boy Scouts a guided tour of the woods.
(57, 58)

6. (Who, Whom) did the lifeguard rescue?
(66, 68)

7. (This, This here) pen is mine.
(71)

8. Clumsy Mr. Tripflip survived his fall from the treetop but was a(n) (invalid, hemisphere, wright)
(55) for several weeks.

9. Laurent (cent, sent, scent) Vincent a postcard from Austria.
(77)

10. Shane lives in a(n) (antifreeze, suburb, rite) of Los Angeles.
(80)

11. Does Victoria know (ware, wear, where) Aimee lives?
(72)

12. Vincent discovered that the (consequence, icon, ware) of not sleeping is fatigue.
(76)

13. Circle each helping verb in this sentence: I should have been resting all day yesterday.
(9)

14. Circle each letter that should be capitalized below.
(6, 29)

     dear mr. streeton,

       thank you for helping at westfield elementary school's
     recent food drive. we surpassed our goal by ten percent!

        sincerely,

        ms. francine farmer

15. Underline the two prepositional phrases in this sentence, and circle the object of each
(17, 33) preposition:

     A person born on February 29 in a leap year has a birthday only every four years.

16. Circle the predicate nominative in this sentence: James Madison was the first president who did
(41) not wear knee breeches.

For 17–19, refer to this sentence: Because Americans supported the French Revolution, they adopted the trousers of the revolutionaries.

17. Underline the independent clause with one line.
(61)

18. Underline the dependent clause with two lines.
(61)

19. Circle the subordinating conjunction.
(61)

20. From the list below, circle the indefinite pronoun that can be either singular or plural:
(72)

several   another   most   many   few   no one

21. Add quotation marks to this sentence:
(69, 70)

Mr. Landis explained, It was actually Beau Brummell who popularized trousers in England.

22. Underline each word that should be italicized in this sentence:
(73)

Treasure Island, a novel by Robert Louis Stevenson, remains a favorite classic.

Add correct punctuation marks to sentences 23 and 24.

23. Peter lives at 52 N Cedar Ave Utica New York
(40, 47)

24. She may decide to leave or she may stay here
(64)

25. Diagram this sentence in the space to the right:
(23, 25) James Madison wore long trousers.

Give after Lesson 90.

Circle the correct words to complete sentences 1–13.

1. Blood flows away from the heart through an artery; it flows toward the heart through a (vane,
(82) vain, vein).

2. The soldier received a special (mettle, medal, metal) for his bravery during the war.
(85)

3. My cousin has (live, lives, lived) in the East all her life.
(78)

4. The 1930s (brung, brought, bringed) a period of hardship and poverty known as the Great
(74) Depression.

5. Tweezers (was, were) used to pull the splinter out of Francisco's finger.
(78, 81)

6. The old horse was galloping (good, well) this morning.
(85)

7. Samara and Chris had a (good, well) horseback ride through the forest.
(85)

8. Write the plural of *family*. _____
(13, 14)

9. Another word for loyalty is (reconcile, allegiance, metal).
(81)

10. We might (imply, infer, heal) from Josephine's smile that she is happy today.
(79)

11. Are you (already, all ready) to take your dictation test?
(83)

12. I hoped that Mr. Tripflip would (heel, heal) quickly.
(84)

13. Kristina is (anxious, eager) to chat with her best friend after school.
(78)

14. Circle the present perfect verb phrase in this sentence:
(19)

Finally, Fred has memorized forty-two simple prepositions.

15. Underline each prepositional phrase in this sentence, and circle the object of each preposition:
(17, 33)

Historians still argue about the cause of the Great Depression.

16. Circle each letter that should be capitalized in this sentence:
(6, 29)

in our history class, miss casey talked about the effect of the great depression in the east.

17. Circle the verb in this sentence, and circle to show whether it is transitive or intransitive:
(32, 2)

Did you proofread your social studies report on the Great Depression? (transitive, intransitive)

18. Add commas as needed to this sentence: During the Great Depression factories produced more
(47, 56) than was demanded and workers lost their jobs as a result.

19. Circle the nominative case pronoun in this sentence: "They invested their money too heavily in
(55) the stock market," Miss Casey told us.

Add quotation marks if needed to sentences 20 and 21.

20. Ernie said, I am very careful with money because I lived through the Great Depression.
(69, 70)

21. Simple Simon is a rhyme from the *Mother Goose* collection.
(70)

22. Circle the word(s) that should be italicized in this sentence:
(73)

Have you ever read the novel Black Beauty?

23. Insert a dash where it is needed in this sentence: Sophie finished reading *Gone with the Wind*
(77) quickly in less than three days.

24. Add hyphens as needed in this sentence: Oops, I added one fourth cup of cinnamon instead of
(86) one fourth teaspoon!

25. Diagram this sentence in the space below: This was another reason for the Great Depression.
(44, 59)

Circle the correct words to complete sentences 1–13.

1. The lost bear (past, passed) by the runner before lumbering back into the wilderness.
(88)

2. A person under the age of twenty-one is labeled a (miner, minor).
(87)

3. Some people (looks, look) for someone else to blame for their misery.
(78, 81)

4. The political (partys, parties) accused each other of leading the country in the wrong direction.
(13)

5. Some people believed that President Roosevelt was (more, most) caring than President Hoover.
(91)

6. Is the car running (good, well) today?
(85)

7. The word "not" is an (adjective, adverb).
(82, 90)

8. The brown squirrel buried (its, it's) acorn.
(15, 60)

9. Six-year-old Kevin has two (loose, lose, loss) teeth.
(89)

10. Sometimes an old wooden floor will (creek, creak) when you walk on it.
(86)

11. Please read the story (allowed, aloud) so that we can all enjoy it.
(90)

12. Grandma's bicycle doesn't move; it is (stationary, stationery).
(73)

13. One of Justin's admirable qualities is his (humility, arrogance). He is not overly proud.
(70)

14. In the blanks below, write the four principal parts of the verb *snore*.
(16)

    (a) present tense:_____   (b) present participle:_____

    (c) past tense:_____   (d) past participle:_____

15. Circle each letter that should be capitalized in this sentence, and underline each word that should
(6, 20) be italicized:

    aunt charlene asked, "do you know, cousin harley, who took my copy of david
    copperfield by charles dickens?"

16. Circle the appositive in this sentence: The next President after Herbert Hoover was a Democrat,
(48) Franklin Delano Roosevelt.

17. Add commas as needed in this sentence: Jordan asked "Did you know Carey that during the
(56, 65) Great Depression people ridiculed President Herbert Hoover?"

18. Circle the negative in this sentence: Did nobody believe that Hoover was doing all he could to
(82) help Americans during the Great Depression?

Add hyphens where they are needed in sentences 19 and 20.

19. Thirty seven cows watched a fast moving train disappear into the night.
(86)

20. Some parents do not allow their children to watch R rated movies.
(86)

For 21 and 22, circle to show whether the italicized word is an adjective or an adverb.

21. That was a *hard* problem. (adjective, adverb)
(27, 84)

22. The math student worked *hard* on the problem. (adjective, adverb)
(27, 84)

Diagram sentences 23–25 in the space to the right.

23. Many Americans blamed Herbert Hoover.
(23, 25)

24. The human suffering during the Great
(34, 44) Depression seemed limitless.

25. That salesperson might have been working too long.
(23, 95)

Circle the correct words to complete sentences 1–11.

1. The baker (peared, pared, paired) the apples and pears before placing them in the unbaked pie
(94) crust.

2. My lost friend did not know (whether, weather) to turn right or left.
(91)

3. Little Boy Blue has (blow, blew, blown) his horn several times already.
(92)

4. Can't (nobody, anybody) find the boy who is in charge of the sheep and cattle?
(82, 98)

5. Franklin Delano Roosevelt and his wife, Eleanor, (was, were) good leaders during difficult times.
(15, 78)

6. Robert, you have sneezed repeatedly; are you feeling (well, good) today?
(85)

7. Leslie (blew, blue) up twenty-six red balloons.
(92)

8. My (deer, dear) Aunt Sue baked me a cherry pie.
(93)

9. Unfortunately, our camp (site, cite, sight) had no trees to offer shade.
(95)

10. After surgery, Mr. Tripflip was not (allowed, aloud) to climb trees for six weeks.
(90)

11. The (weather, whether) (vane, vain, vein) indicates that the wind is blowing from the north.
(91, 82)

12. Circle each letter that should be capitalized in this sentence:
(6, 12)

        on monday, i asked, "where is the boy who looks after the sheep?"

13. Underline the prepositional phrase, and circle the object of the preposition in this sentence:
(17, 33)

        The sheep are grazing in the meadow.

14. Add periods as they are needed in this sentence: Little Boy Blue blew his horn at 8 am daily
(36, 40)

15. Circle the predicate nominative in this sentence:
(41)

        Little Boy Blue was the sleepy young man under the haystack.

16. Add commas as they are needed in this sentence:
(49)

        Where were you Little Boy Blue while the animals were escaping?

17. Circle the personal pronoun in this sentence, and circle to show whether the pronoun is first,
(58) second, or third person:

Did you know that, in the 1880s, schools were established for Native Americans? (1st, 2nd, 3rd person)

18. Circle the reflexive personal pronoun in this sentence:
(62)

When she returned home from school, Little Dove busied herself with the household chores.

For 19–21, refer to this sentence: Although Native Americans gained knowledge in these schools, they lost much of their tribal heritage.

19. Underline the dependent clause with one line.
(61)

20. Underline the independent clause with two lines.
(61)

21. Circle the subordinating conjunction.
(61)

22. Circle to show whether the italicized word in each sentence is an adjective or an adverb.
(44, 89)

(a) Her departure was *early*. (adjective, adverb) (b) She departed *early*. (adjective, adverb)

23. Write the comparison forms for the irregular adverb *badly*.
(91)

positive ___badly___ comparative _____ superlative _____

24. Insert a colon where it is needed in this sentence:
(94)

The cheese spread contains these ingredients butter, garlic, romano cheese, and parmesan cheese.

25. Diagram the following sentence in the space below: Now, Native Americans can learn Navajo
(87, 95) language and history at school.

Give after Lesson 105.

Circle the correct words to complete sentences 1–11.

1. Flowers that bloom year after year are called (biannuals, perennials, semiannuals).
(96)

2. The photographer brought a (toxin, triangle, tripod) to support his camera.
(97)

3. A dependent clause may be connected to an independent clause by a (coordinating,
(61) subordinating) conjunction.

4. The sentence below is (simple, compound, complex, compound-complex).
(99)

　　　　　The pronoun patrol apprehended me because I used the word "hisself."

5. Down the hill (come, comes) Jill.
(78, 79)

6. This sentence is (active, passive) voice: Jack broke his crown.
(100)

7. The prefix (*tri-, anti-, homo-*) means "against."
(65)

8. After (sometime, some time, sometimes) had passed, Mr. Tripflip felt better.
(102)

9. *Loyalty* and (*frugality, fidelity, patience*) have almost the same meaning.
(103)

10. *Truth* and (*verity, forbearance, frugality*) have almost the same meaning.
(100)

11. Daniel and Mark do not waste money; they are (homonyms, frugal, ultramodern).
(105)

12. Add periods as needed to this sentence: On Sunday morning, Dec 7, 1941, the Japanese bombed
(36, 40) Pearl Harbor

13. Add commas as needed to this sentence: Hey Grandpa I think Jack plastered his head with
(49, 56) vinegar and brown paper.

14. Circle the four subordinating conjunctions in this list: since, over, while, jump, in order that,
(61) camera, although, anxious

15. Add quotation marks to this sentence: After the bombing, millions of young men flocked to the
(69) military crying, Remember Pearl Harbor!

Add hyphens where they are needed in sentences 16 and 17.

16. Antoine treasured his paint stained overalls.
(86)

17. Two thirds of the world's eggplant is grown in New Jersey.
(86)

18. Circle the adverb in this sentence: Immediately, President Roosevelt declared war on Japan.
(89)

Circle the correct part of speech for the italicized word in sentences 19 and 20.

19. The manatee rolled *over*. (adverb, preposition)
(96)

20. The manatee rolled *over* me. (adverb, preposition)
(96)

Add apostrophes where they are needed in sentences 21 and 22.

21. Charlie said, "Ive been talkin to the old fisherman since six oclock this mornin."
(97)

22. Its amazing to me that in the year 01, there were fewer people than chickens.
(97)

23. Add a semicolon and an apostrophe where they are needed in this sentence:
(92, 98)

Delilahs answer was correct the longest one-syllable word is *screeched*.

24. Add a colon where it is needed in this sentence: Christie told me a curious fact "The flag
(94) pictured on a Canadian two-dollar bill is an American flag."

25. Diagram this sentence in the space below: A dragonfly normally lives for a few weeks.
(23, 95)

Give after Lesson 107.

Circle the correct words to complete sentences 1–9.

1. While conscientiousness and diligence are desirable character traits, (punctuality,
(107)   procrastination, perseverance) is not.

2. The giving of one's time, talents, and money is an example of (generosity, sympathy, willpower).
(106)

3. They (was, were) diligent, hard-working students.
(78, 81)

4. I cannot (conceive, concieve) of a person sailing in a bowl.
(107)

5. The prefix (*uni-*, *re-*, *poly-*) means "again."
(99)

6. A doe is a female (dear, deer).
(93)

7. Last night's sunset was a beautiful (site, cite, sight).
(95)

8. The prefix (*uni-*, *poly-*, *tri-*) means "three."
(97)

9. Justin shares freely. He is (frugal, patient, generous) and unselfish.
(106)

10. Circle the helping verb in this sentence: John Scott Harrison was born in Indiana in 1804.
(9)

11. Circle the linking verb in this sentence: John Scott Harrison was the son of William Henry
(22)   Harrison, the ninth President of the United States; and the father of Benjamin Harrison, the
twenty-third President.

12. Write the plural of each noun: turkey _____   tray _____
(13)

                  boss _____   puppy _____

13. Circle each letter that should be capitalized in this rhyme:
(6, 12)

                     three wise men of gothan
                     went to sea in a bowl.
                     if the bowl had been stronger,
                     my song would have been longer.

14. Circle each letter that should be capitalized in this outline, and add periods as needed:
(20)

                i flowers
                  a annuals
                  b perennials

15. Circle the possessive pronoun in this sentence: They thought the bowl was theirs.
(60)

16. Circle the demonstrative pronoun in this sentence: That was their silly mode of transportation.
(71)

17. Circle each adverb in this sentence: The three wise men of Gothan happily sailed everywhere.
(84, 87)

18. Add a colon where it is needed in this sentence: Sometimes I misspell these words receive,
(94) separate, etc.

19. Write the possessive form of each of these plural nouns:
(97)

      turkeys _____   students _____

      winners _____   mice _____

20. Write the four principal parts of the verb *break*.
(16)

    (a) present tense:_____   (b) present participle:_____

    (c) past tense:_____   (d) past participle:_____

For 21–24, refer to this sentence: Three men went to sea in a bowl, but they didn't have much luck.

21. Underline the first independent clause.
(37)

22. Circle the second independent clause.
(37, 61)

23. Draw a box around the coordinating conjunction.
(37, 61)

24. Diagram the sentence in the space below: Three men went to sea in a bowl, but they didn't have
(87, 95) much luck.

25. Diagram the following sentence in the space below: Yes, he gave me the address.
(35, 102)

Circle the correct words to complete sentences 1–10.

1. A person with allergies is aided by a group of medicines called (homophones, antihistamines,
(101) hemiplegia).

2. The poison, or toxin, of a black widow spider can be neutralized with an (antitoxin, antiseptic,
(101) hemistich).

3. The sentence below is (simple, compound, complex).
(99)
Even though it doesn't make any difference, cows are always milked from the right side,
probably because most people are right-handed.

4. The farmer (saw, seen, sawed) his mistake when he attempted to milk the cow from the left side.
(75, 78)

5. He didn't eat (anything, nothing) besides a banana before school.
(82)

6. Laurent wore a (pare, pear, pair) of shiny black shoes to the concert.
(94)

7. The prefix (*uni-*, *geo-*, *hemi-*) means "half."
(67)

8. Silver is a lustrous (metal, mettle, medal) used for coins, tableware, jewelry, etc.
(85)

9. Delay and postponement are similar to (generosity, procrastination, antitoxin).
(106, 107)

10. Josephine likes the sunshine and (blew, blue) sky in Southern California.
(92)

11. Write the four principal parts of the verb *grip*.
(16, 106)

    (a) present tense:_____   (b) present participle:_____

    (c) past tense:_____   (d) past participle:_____

12. Circle the appositive in this sentence: The pumpkin eater, Peter, had a wife but couldn't take
(48) care of her.

13. Circle each letter that should be capitalized in this sentence: hey, grandpa, why did peter put his
(6, 12) wife into a pumpkin on tuesday?

Add commas where they are needed in sentences 14 and 15.

14. Well if Peter put his wife into a pumpkin he could keep her from harm.
(56)

15. She would be safe and he would be happy.
(65)

16. Circle the objective case pronoun in this sentence: She wished that he wouldn't keep her as a
(57) prisoner.

17. Circle the nominative case pronoun in this sentence: Did he actually lock her inside the pumpkin?
(56)

18. Circle the possessive case pronoun in this sentence: She insisted the pumpkin was not his.
(60)

19. Use a hyphen to divide the word *president* as you would at the end of a line. _____
(88)

20. Underline the prepositional phrase used as an adverb in this sentence, and circle the word it
(17, 95) modifies:

Most Americans live within fifty miles of their birthplace.

21. Add a semicolon where it is needed in this sentence: An ostrich has large eyes they are bigger than
(92) its brain.

22. Write the possessive form of each noun or noun pair.
(97)

Keats _____   grandparents _____

Scot and Debby (their dog) _____   Mr. Fox _____

23. Circle the interjection in this sentence: Oh yes, bullet-proof vests and fire escapes were both
(102) invented by women.

24. Circle each silent letter in these words: match   walk   numb   wrist   knew
(103, 104)

25. Diagram this sentence: Peter was poor but innovative.
(23, 44)